Assert Yourself!

Behavior Modification Series

Behavior Modification in Residential Treatment of Children
  Pizzat, F., Ph.D.
The Behavioral Treatment of Psychotic Illness
  DiScipio, W., Ph.D. Editor
Constructive Classroom Behavior
  Sarason, G., Ph.D. and Sarason, B.R., Ph.D.
Reinforcing Productive Classroom Behavior
  Glaser, M., Ph.D. and Fargo, G.A., Ph.D.
Living in the Classroom
  Payne, J.S., Ed.D., Polloway, E.A., Kauffman, J.M., Ed.D. and Scranton, T.R., Ed.D.
Assert Yourself! How to Be Your Own Person
  Galassi, M.D., Ed.D. and Galassi, J.P., Ph.D.

Assert Yourself!
How to Be Your Own Person

Merna Dee Galassi
and
John P. Galassi

HUMAN SCIENCES PRESS
Formerly BEHAVIORAL PUBLICATIONS INC.
72 FIFTH AVENUE, NEW YORK, N.Y. 10011

Library of Congress Catalog Number 76-57936

ISBN: 0-87705-299-9

Copyright © 1977 by Human Sciences Press 72 Fifth Avenue, New York, New York 10011

All rights reserved. No part of this work may be reproduced or utilized in any form or by any means, electronic or mechanical, including photocopying, microfilm and recording, or by any information storage and retrieval system without permission in writing from the publisher.

Printed in the United States of America
789 987654321

Library of Congress Cataloging in Publication Data
Main entry under title
   Galassi, Merna Dee.
     Assert yourself.

      1. Assertiveness (Psychology) I. Galassi, John P., joint author. II. Title.
BF575.A85G34   158'.1   76-57936

To our parents
Leroy and Shirley
John and Anna

Contents

Acknowledgements ... viii

Introduction ... ix
    Overview for the Self-Help User ... x
    Overview for the Trainer ... xii

Chapter One: Fundamentals of Assertion ... 1
    1. Assertive Behavior ... 3
        Definition, Importance, and Development, 3;
        Assessing Your Behavior, 7.
    2. Assertive, Aggressive, and Nonassertive Behavior ... 14
        Recognizing, 14; Discriminating, 19.
    3. Assertion Training and Assertive Behavior ... 30
        Procedures and Criteria, 30; Rating Anxiety
        and Verbal Content, 55.
    4. Assertion Training Programs ... 70
        Deep Muscle Relaxation, 70; Personalizing
        Your Program, 75.

Chapter Two: Expressing Positive Feelings ... 81
    5. Giving and Receiving Compliments ... 83
    6. Making Requests ... 97
    7. Expressing Liking, Love, and Affection ... 104
    8. Initiating and Maintaining Conversations ... 111

Chapter Three: Self-Affirmation ... 121
    9. Standing Up For Your Legitimate Rights ... 123
    10. Refusing Requests ... 133
    11. Expressing Personal Opinions ... 142

Chapter Four: Expressing Negative Feelings ... 151
    12. Expressing Justified Annoyance and Displeasure ... 153
    13. Expressing Justified Anger ... 162

Chapter Five: Assertion in Special Situations and with Special People ... 171
    14. Assertion with Parents and Other Family Members ... 173
    15. Assertion with Authority Figures ... 182
    16. Assertion in Couples ... 190
    17. Assertion in Work Situations ... 199
    18. Assertion for College Students ... 208

Chapter Six: Concluding Remarks ... 219

Appendix A: Additional Trainer Considerations: Assertion for Children ... 222

Appendix B: Principles for Ethical Practice of Assertive Behavior Training ... 231

Acknowledgements

We would like to thank several people who helped us improve the content and format of the manual. First, we appreciate the help of three assertion training leaders, students, and friends—Alice Lawler, Steve Mullinix, and Ann Willson—who freely devoted an untold number of hours to reading and evaluating the manual. We express special thanks to Alice and Steve for their comments on organization, content, and style, and to Ann for her suggestions on practice and for field-testing a draft of the manual.

Finally, we would like to express our appreciation to Mary Anne Fisher, who not only typed the manuscript but also contributed in many areas of its development. Thank you for comments on organization, style, content, and for generally making sure we kept on schedule.

Introduction

Assertion training has gained much recognition in the last few years. Many individuals have improved their self-expression skills through assertion training, and educators and mental health professionals have incorporated this training into their teaching and counseling. This manual has been designed to meet the needs of a variety of users. It can be used as a self-help manual by the individual who wants to learn to become more assertive on his or her own. It also can serve as a manual to help mental health professionals and educators develop individual and group assertion training programs. Finally, it can be used as a manual by members of an assertion training group or class.

In response to the different needs of our readers, two separate overviews of the manual are provided. The first overview, which immediately follows, is designed for the self-help user. It also can be read by group members to provide an orientation to the manual. The second overview to the manual, on page xii, is addressed to those who are planning to develop assertion training programs for their trainees or students.

Overview for the Self-Help User

This manual has been designed to teach people how to express a variety of personal opinions, feelings, and attitudes in a more effective and socially appropriate manner. Such training is often called assertion training, assertive training, assertiveness training, assertive behavior training, social skills training, and personal effectiveness training. We have attempted to write a book on assertion training that is complete for the self-help user and that is based on research data that have demonstrated the effectiveness of these procedures in helping people to become more assertive in their daily lives.

Assertion training is concerned both with helping people who have difficulty in expressing themselves to behave assertively and with helping people who are aggressive in their daily interactions to learn to express themselves in an assertive and therefore acceptable manner. To enable you to become more assertive, we describe throughout the manual techniques designed to help you change your verbal and nonverbal behaviors as well as techniques designed to help you change attitudes and beliefs that may interfere with behaving assertively. We believe that learning to behave assertively is an important skill to develop. As with other skills, such as tennis or golf, it requires systematic practice. At times, you may find that learning assertive behavior on your own is difficult, and you may want to seek help from a qualified skills teacher such as a counselor or a psychologist. We believe that it is important to seek help when you feel it is necessary, and Appendix B discusses some of the qualifications that are important to assess when you are seeking a qualified trainer.

In using this manual, we believe that it is important that you read Chapter One thoroughly. Chapter One presents the basic theory, philosophy, and methods of assertion training that you will use throughout the remainder of the manual. In addition, it contains a procedure by which you can determine for yourself the specific areas in which you may profit the most from assertion training.

Once you have determined the areas of assertive behavior in which you would like to improve your skills, you then can turn to the corresponding discussion and exercise modules in Chapters Two through Five and begin your own unique assertion training program. Each of these later chapters consists of several matched pairs of discussion and exercise modules. Each discussion module contains important material about the rights, responsibilities, and rationale for a particular behavior—expressing personal opinions, for example. Each discussion module is followed by an exercise module that describes situations that will give you practice in expressing yourself more assertively in the particular behavior. As you proceed, you may find that there are some discussion and exercise modules to which you will devote little or no attention and other modules on which you concentrate a great deal of effort. The important thing is to determine the areas in which you would like to improve your behavior and then to proceed systematically through the corresponding discussion and exercise modules.

Learning to behave assertively does not occur over night. It takes time and hard work. During the process, you may become disappointed in yourself; you may find that your progress is slower than you like and that you need more practice than you anticipated. As in learning any skill, you will improve if you are motivated and willing to try out new behaviors. We hope that you enjoy our program and that you profit from it. At this point, we suggest that you turn to Chapter One and begin your program on page 3.

Good luck with your training.

Overview for the Trainer

This manual is designed to help educators, human development specialists, and mental health professionals to develop assertion training programs. Such programs may be useful with a wide variety of populations, including students, women's groups, business personnel, mental health clients, and adults in general and in a number of settings, including schools, colleges, community mental health centers, and psychiatric hospitals. The manual can be used in either group or individual assertion training programs.
It is an outgrowth of successful clinical practice and research designed to teach assertive behavior to individuals who had difficulty expressing themselves (Galassi, 1973; Galassi, Galassi & Litz, 1974; Galassi, Kostka & Galassi, 1975), and is designed to help individuals who lack assertive skills as well as those who often are aggressive to behave in an assertive manner.

HOW TO USE THIS MANUAL

The manual consists of six chapters, each divided into a series of exercise and discussion modules. Each exercise module consists of a number of experiences designed to involve the trainee in the development of assertive behaviors. Most of the exercises can be responded to in either a written or a role-playing format. The discussion modules provide the trainee with the needed conceptual and practical understanding of assertive behavior that is necessary for a successful training program.

With the exception of Chapter One, it is not imperative that each chapter be used in its entirety or in a prescribed order. Rather, the exercise and discussion modules in subsequent chapters may be combined and sequenced in in a variety of ways, based on the preliminary assessment of assertive behavior detailed in Chapter One. Before responding to the exercises in Chapters Two through Five, the trainee should familiarize himself/herself with the rights and responsibilities imposed by the demands of these everyday situations as presented in the accompanying discussion modules in each of these chapters. We hope that the provision of a number of these self-contained modules will permit maximum flexibility for you.

It is strongly recommended that the modules in Chapter One be considered first, since they present the fundamental concepts of assertive behavior and assertion training. Then sequencing can depend on the situations or individuals which pose special difficulties for trainees. For example, college students, adults living at home, and newlyweds often experience particular difficulties asserting themselves with parents. Chapter Five provides discussion and exercise modules for these and other special situations.

TRAINER CONSIDERATIONS IN ORGANIZING AND IMPLEMENTING ASSERTION TRAINING PROGRAMS

One of the primary considerations you face as a trainer is to be able to assert yourself consistently and to be comfortable with behaving in this manner. If you are not skilled in assertive behavior or are not comfortable with it, then you may encounter difficulty in teaching your trainees to assert themselves and in answering their questions or responding to the apprehensions they may express. Remember that your behavior serves as a model for your trainees. Because of the importance of being comfortable with assertive behavior, we suggest that you complete the self-contained program before using it with others. In addition, recognizing that assertion is quite different from aggression and that the rights of others are as important as the rights of the asserting person, it is our hope that this program will be used responsibly and carefully. Trainers should be able to recognize whether counseling or some form of additional help may be indicated for a trainee. Trainers also need to be aware of their own professional qualifications and limitations. In this regard, Appendix B may prove useful.

Other important considerations in training include assessment, group size and composition, session length and format, and general training strategies.

Assessment

Assessment is an integral part of any learning process, whether you are helping an individual to learn to read, to play an instrument, to speak fluently, to reduce his anxiety, or to behave assertively. As a result, you will probably find it quite useful to assess the assertive behavior of your trainees before, during, and after training. In addition to the general screening procedures that you presently use, an assessment of assertion before training will provide information about the types of behaviors and the persons with whom your trainees have difficulty in asserting themselves. This information will enable you to construct and select relevant modules from Chapters Two through Five that will be of maximum benefit to your trainees. An initial assessment combined with feedback to the trainees will help to orient them to the need for assertion training and to the areas in which they may want to improve their skills of self-expression. Assessment after training will provide feedback about the progress that the trainees have made and alert them to areas in which they may need additional practice.

An instrument for assessing assertive behavior is included in Chapter One. The Assertion Self-Assessment Table is comprehensive and provides information on the frequency with which an individual asserts himself/herself as well as information on the level of difficulty experienced during self-assertion and the situations in which an individual may behave aggressively. We suggest that you complete this assessment in order to evaluate your own skills of self-assertion and to determine the best way to use this assessment with your trainees.

If you prefer instruments for assessing behavior that have been subjected to validation, we recommend the Adult Self-Expression Scale, available from Adult Self-Expression Scale, P.O. Box 17174, Charlotte, N.C. 28211, and the College Self-Expression Scale (Galassi, DeLo, Galassi, and Bastien, *Behavior Therapy, 5,* 1974, 165-171). You may also wish to assess your trainees' level of aggressive behavior. One instrument that may be helpful for this purpose is the Buss-Durkee Inventory (Buss & Durkee, *Journal of Consulting Psychology, 21,* 1957, 343-349). Material in this manual can be used to help both individuals who assert themselves infrequently and individuals who act aggressively to behave in an assertive manner.

Group Size and Composition

This assertion training manual can be used with groups of different sizes by making minor procedural modifications. It can be used with large groups such as classes, small groups such as counseling groups and human growth or psychotherapy groups, and with dyads such as husband and wife or other pairings as well as with single individuals. The size of your group should be determined by both the goals of your members and the particular needs of your population.

Individuals and Couples

Assertion training was developed originally for use by counselors or therapists with individual trainees, clients, or patients. It relies quite heavily on learning theory and the use of behavior rehearsal or role playing to teach an individual new behaviors. In behavior rehearsal, the trainer or counselor plays the role of a person with whom the trainee has difficulty asserting himself/herself. The trainee plays himself/herself and rehearses the role several times until he/she is more comfortable and more skilled with his/her new behavior. Occasionally the roles are reversed so that the trainer can be certain that he/she is reproducing accurately the behavior of the person with whom the trainee has difficulty. Throughout behavior rehearsal, the trainer provides critical feedback to the trainee on his/her behavior and corrects any misconceptions or counterproductive beliefs that are preventing the client from asserting himself/herself.

This manual can be used in the manner just described with individual trainees. The assertion training criteria in Chapter One provide you with a systematic way of providing feedback to your clients. The exercise modules and the instructions for developing individualized exercises provide an ample number of situations for rehearsal. Finally, the discussion modules on rights, responsibilities, and rationale present information that is helpful in changing misconceptions and counterproductive beliefs.

When using this manual with couples, a few minor procedural modifications can be made. Behavior rehearsal can take place between the members of the couple with you providing feedback to the member of the couple who is practicing assertive behavior at that time. You also can call upon the other member of the couple to provide feedback. In addition, it is possible to have both members of the couple rehearse an assertive interaction simultaneously. For example, one member of the couple may practice giving a compliment in an assertive manner while the other member rehearses accepting the compliment assertively. Thus you are teaching the couple to restructure their communication pattern. Misconceptions by one or both members of the couple can be corrected on the spot.

Small Groups

In working with small groups, minor procedural modifications once again may be desirable. You may want to divide the members of your group into dyads or triads for behavior rehearsal.

If a triad is used, one member can practice assertive behavior; the second member can serve as the individual who is the target of assertive behavior; and the third member can observe and evaluate the interaction, using the assertion training criteria in Chapter One. Subsequently, the triad members can rotate their roles. If a dyad is used, the second member of the dyad will serve as the critic as well as the target of assertive behavior. You can circulate among the triads (dyads) checking the progress of the members, providing feedback and coaching, and correcting counterproductive beliefs or misconceptions. A segment of the session might be used to discuss concerns about the rights, responsibilities, and rationale of assertive behavior and to discuss the successes and failures that group members have had in asserting themselves outside of the group. In our experience, a group that consists of eight to twelve members working in dyads or triads and led by two trainers has been quite successful.

Large Groups or Classes

In large groups, you probably will find that it is more efficient to use behavior rehearsal with triads rather than dyads. Since it is unlikely that you will be able to observe every triad, a question and answer period might be useful following each behavior rehearsal. In this segment, individuals can raise questions that occurred during behavior rehearsal. Your responses to these questions undoubtedly would constitute useful information for the group as a whole.

Because of noise levels and physical space limitations in the large group setting, it may be useful to rely on modeling or observational learning to a greater extent than experiential learning. For example, rather than having the whole class participate in behavior rehearsal, you can have one or two volunteer members rehearse and receive feedback on an exercise while the remainder of the group observes and records the desirable and undesirable behaviors using the assertion training criteria. You can ask individual class members to provide feedback or raise questions. The material contained in the discussion modules on rights, responsibilities, and rationale can be presented in lecture format.

Number, Length, and Format of Sessions

The exact number of sessions and length of each will have to be determined by your time constraints and the needs of your population. In general, we feel that the format of the session is crucial. We have found that the most successful format includes a mixture of group discussion and role playing during each session. This combination tends to keep all members involved and requires each member to focus on his/her own behavior in concrete rather than abstract terms.

The number and length of sessions will vary according to the amount of discussion you have arising from the discussion modules, the members' reactions to their role-playing performance, and the number of exercises you feel are necessary for your particular group members to rehearse.

You can use the manual to construct assertion training programs varying in length from one-half day and weekend-long workshops to groups that meet weekly for periods of up to ten weeks or longer. With groups that are abbreviated in length, it is helpful for the members to read the material in Chapter One and to complete the assessment instrument prior to the first group meeting. In the event that this is not possible, you can present the fundamentals of Chapter One in condensed form through a lecture.

An assertion training program that we have found quite productive consists of one-and-a-half to two-hour sessions twice a week for four weeks or once a week for eight weeks. Each session is divided into three more or less equivalent segments. The first segment is a discussion segment and is followed by two behavior rehearsal segments in which group members practice both standard and individually constructed exercises. An example of the first session of this program is outlined below.

Session One

1. Prior to the first session, complete the assertion instrument in Exercise Module 1.
2. Introduction of members and trainer(s). Getting acquainted activities or warm-up exercises may be used at this point, if desired.
3. Trainer presents an overview of the material in Discussion Module 1 followed by group discussion.
4. Trainer presents overview of Discussion Module 3 followed by group discussion.
5. Behavior Rehearsal: One situation from Exercise Module 6, Making Requests, plus a short discussion on rights, responsibilities, and rationale for this behavior.
6. Behavior Rehearsal: One situation from Exercise Module 9, Expressing Legitimate Rights, plus a short discussion on rights, responsibilities, and rationale for this behavior.
7. Homework: Read Discussion Module 1, to be discussed in more detail at Session 2. Read Discussion Module 2, to be discussed at Session 2. Begin keeping a Daily Log of Assertive Behavior in Naturally Occurring Interactions (Table 3).

Again, the format, length, and number of sessions should be dictated by your time constraints and an assessment of the needs of your population. Given this information, you should plug in the most relevant exercise and discussion modules from Chapter One and the remainder of this manual.

GENERAL TRAINING STRATEGIES

The following is a list of general training strategies that we recommend you incorporate into your assertion training programs.

1. Trainees who are deficient in assertive behavior often will be hesitant to engage in assertive responses and will become easily discouraged if they are not immediately successful. As a result, it is important for you to provide frequent and sincere verbal praise for even first approximations of assertive behavior by the trainee during behavior rehearsal. It is important to increase both the trainee's skills and confidence. Emphasize what is positive in the trainee's performance.
2. During behavior rehearsal, praise the trainee for what he/she has done well, then select *one* or *at most two* behaviors to improve at any one time.
3. Give concrete feedback to the trainee by either showing him/her or telling him/her what you would like him/her to do. It is particularly important during the early training phases to tell the trainee exactly what to say.
4. Video and/or audiotape feedback are quite useful in assertion training programs. Through these media, an individual learns to observe and evaluate his/her own behavior and receives constant reinforcement when he/she views himself/herself demonstrating appropriate assertive behavior. In addition, you can use video or audiotape to prepare and present short models of assertive interactions to the group. You could tape some of the models we have provided throughout the manual.

5. When working with mixed-sex groups, it often is helpful to use behavior rehearsal with like-sexed dyads or triads for the first few sessions and then to progress to opposite-sex rehearsals during the later sessions. Most trainees find that it is less anxiety provoking to learn to assert themselves with persons of the same sex initially. Thus, beginning with same sex dyads or triads helps to maintain trainees' anxiety at manageable levels.
6. It is important that trainees understand that changes in their behavior may affect their relationship with their families, friends, and associates. Trainees who have previously allowed others to make their decisions for them or who have been willing to do almost anything that a spouse or friend demanded may find that the significant others are not only shocked by their new behavior but also displeased—at least initially. Therefore, we recommend that trainees inform significant others in their environment that they are learning to behave assertively and that this may involve changes in their relationships. Trainees might be encouraged to ask these significant others for feedback and support in their efforts to develop new behaviors. You may suggest that trainees ask family members and close friends to read excerpts from the manual in order to help them understand more clearly what is involved in assertion training.
7. For many trainees, anxiety related to self-assertion will be reduced during repeated behavior rehearsals. However, some trainees may be generally anxious or experience an unusual amount of anxiety in expressing themselves assertively. This will be particularly true for those of you who are leading counseling or therapy groups or who are working in hospital settings. It may be necessary to teach generally anxious or excessively anxious trainees deep-muscle relaxation or to use systematic desensitization with respect to anxiety concerning self-assertion. Exercise Module 4 describes the relaxation procedures. Additional information on relaxation and systematic desensitization can be found in Wolpe (1973). See the supplemental readings listed below.
8. It is appropriate and imperative for you to dispute directly counterproductive attitudes and misconceptions that inhibit a trainee from asserting himself/herself. Discussion Modules 3 and 5-18 present many of the typical counterproductive attitudes and misconceptions held by individuals. Ways to deal with these misconceptions and counterproductive attitudes are provided in these discusions modules. Some examples of counterproductive attitudes include:

It is all right for my friends to ask me for favors, but I don't want to impose on them (see Discussion Module 6).
It's kind of silly for a man to express affection verbally (see Discussion Module 7).
I really don't mind doing most of the work (see Discussion Module 15).
Real friends never get angry at each other (see Discussion Module 3).
I really have to have a good reason for telling him I don't want to help him (see Discussion Module 10).

9. It is crucial that trainees learn to clearly distinguish between nonassertive, aggressive, and assertive behavior, and, more importantly, that they be able to reflect such discriminations in their own behavior. If assertion training is to be successful, it is extremely important that trainees learn assertive, *not* aggressive, ways of interacting.
10. Exercise Module 2, Discriminating Nonassertive, Aggressive, and Assertive Behavior, and the section in Exercise Module 3 on Rating Verbal Content either can be used as homework assignments or can be presented to the group and then rated. If these exercises are read aloud or presented on tape, nonverbal behaviors and tone of voice can be added to emphasize the meaning being expressed.

11. Appendix A provides information on using assertion training with children.

This section on trainer considerations has been deliberately kept to a minimum since much of the explanatory material has been included in the manual modules. We suggest that you study the remainder of the manual prior to developing an assertion training program.

SELECTED SUPPLEMENTAL READINGS

Alberti, R.E., and Emmons, M.L. (2nd ed.). *Your Perfect Right: A Guide to Assertive Behavior.* San Luis Obispo: Impact, 1974.

Fensterheim, H., and Baer, J. *Don't Say Yes When You Want to Say No.* New York: David McKay Co., 1975.

Galassi, M.D., and Galassi, J.P. "Assertion: A Critical Review," *Psychotherapy: Theory, Research and Practice,* 1976, in press.

Hersen, M., Eisler, R.M., and Miller, P.M. "Development of Assertive Responses: Clinical Measurement and Research Considerations." *Behaviour Research and Therapy 11*, (1973), 505-521.

Jakubowski-Spector, P. "Facilitating the Growth of Women through Assertive Training," *The Counseling Psychologist 4*(1), (1973), 75-86.

McFall, R.M., and Twentyman, C.T. "Four Experiments on the Relative Contributions of Rehearsal, Modeling, and Coaching to Assertion Training." *Journal of Abnormal Psychology 81* (1973), 199-218.

Phelps, S., and Austin, N. *The Assertive Woman.* San Luis Obispo: Impact, 1975.

Salter, A. *Conditioned Reflex Therapy.* New York: Capricorn Books, 1949. Chapters 5, 6, and 11.

Serber, M. "Teaching the Nonverbal Components of Assertive Training." *Journal of Behavior Therapy and Experimental Psychiatry 3* (1972), 179-183.

Wolpe, J. *The Practice of Behavior Therapy.* New York: Pergamon Press, 1973. Chapters 5 and 6.

REFERENCES

Galassi, J.P. *Assertive Training in Groups Using Video Feedback.* Final progress report on National Institute of Mental Health Small Research Grant MH 22392-01, West Virginia University, 1973.

Galassi, J.P., Galassi, M.D., and Litz, C.M. "Assertive Training in Groups Using Video Feedback." *Journal of Counseling Psychology 21*, (1974), 390-394.

Galassi, J.P., Kostka, M.P., and Galassi, M.D. "Assertive Training: A One Year Follow-up." *Journal of Counseling Psychology 22*, (1975), 451-452.

Chapter 1

Fundamentals of Assertion

In Chapter One, we discuss concepts that are fundamental to an assertion training program. In this chapter, you will learn to identify assertive behavior and to discriminate it from nonassertive and aggressive behavior. You will assess your own skills of self-expression as a preliminary step to constructing an assertion training program. You also will be taught assertion training procedures and criteria for assessing your progress as you proceed through your program. Finally, you will be given instructions on how to construct your assertion training program and how to use the remainder of the manual. We strongly recommend that you read Chapter One in its entirety.

Discussion Module **1**

Definition, Importance, and Development of Assertive Behavior

Definition of Assertive Behavior

Assertive behavior, or assertion, involves direct expression of one's feelings, preferences, needs, or opinions in a manner that is neither threatening nor punishing toward another person. In addition, assertion does not involve an undue or excessive amount of anxiety or fear. Contrary to popular opinion, assertion is not primarily a way to get what one wants, nor is it a way of controlling or subtly manipulating others. Assertion is the direct communication of one's needs, wants, and opinions without punishing, threatening, or putting down the other person. It also involves standing up for one's legitimate rights without violating the rights of others and without being unduly fearful in the process. As such, assertion does not constitute a panacea nor a simple solution for the world's ills but simply is a means of direct and honest communication between individuals. The emphasis is placed on your ability to express your feelings and opinions appropriately.

Assertive behavior should be viewed as a behavior that is both learned and situationally specific. By this we mean that assertion is not something you are born with nor is it something that people either possess—like blue eyes—or do not possess. It is a skill or a way of behaving that one learns; therefore, it can be taught. Also, it is not necessarily a general way of behaving. People are not assertive in all situations. Rather, one learns different types of behavior in different situations. One individual may have difficulty in expressing disagreement with his/her parents but have no difficulty expressing disagreement to friends. In the two situations, the person has learned to behave differently. Another individual may express himself/herself satisfactorily with parents but have difficulty receiving compliments from his/her spouse. Thus you can see that people are not generally assertive or nonassertive but that their behavior varies with the situation.

Assertion consists of a number of behaviors addressed to a variety of people. We have grouped the behaviors under three broad categories: expressing positive feelings, self-affirmation, and expressing negative feelings. Some of the people that play an important role in assertion include friends, spouses or boyfriends and girlfriends, parents and other family members, authority figures, business contacts, and co-workers and subordinates. If you turn to Table 1 in Exercise Module 1, you will see some of the behaviors and people that have an important influence on your self-expression.

As you can see, expressing positive feelings involves giving and receiving compliments, making requests, expressing liking, love, and affection, and initiating and maintaining conversations. Self-affirmation consists of expressing legitimate rights, refusing requests, and expressing personal opinions. Finally, negative feelings involve expressing justified annoyance and displeasure and justified anger.

How often you assert yourself undoubtedly varies within these three broad categories. You probably assert yourself more often with some of the behaviors than with others. For example, you may find it easier to express your annoyance to others than to make requests of them. In addition, you probably express yourself more frequently with some people than with others. Perhaps, it is easier for you to talk to your boss than to your in-laws. As we have said, assertion is not a general way of behaving; it is a skill that we learn and that is related to the situations we encounter. Other factors also influence the likelihood of assertive behavior. Some of these include the cultural setting and the audience present in the situation. These factors influence when assertive behavior is appropriate and what constitutes appropriate behavior.

The exercises in this manual were designed to teach you to express yourself more effectively with a wide variety of assertive behaviors and with a variety of persons whom you encounter from day to day.

Why Is Assertion Important ?

There are a number of reasons why assertion is important. First, the ability to express oneself appears to be a desirable and, at times, necessary skill for human survival. In addition, the ability to express oneself has been an important component of definitions of mental health down through the years. We often find that individuals who have difficulty expressing themselves across a wide variety of behaviors with a number of individuals report feelings of low self-esteem, depression, and undue anxiety in interpersonal situations. They report that they feel unappreciated, taken for granted, or used by others. They often report various somatic or psychosomatic complaints, such as headaches and stomach problems.

In contrast, individuals who have participated in responsible assertion training programs frequently report increased feelings of self-confidence, positive reactions from others, reduced anxiety in social situations, improved interpersonal communication, and decreased somatic complaints. Assertion training is neither a cure-all nor a substitute for counseling; however, many of the by-products mentioned above do occur when one learns to assert oneself. Thus, it would seem that the ability to assert oneself when one so chooses is a desirable skill to master.

Development of Nonassertive and Assertive Ways of Behaving

At this point, you may be wondering how you learned or developed the habit of not asserting yourself in certain situations. There probably is no easy answer to that question, and certainly the answer will be different for each person. However, there are a number of factors, including punishment, reinforcement, modeling, lack of opportunity, cultural standards and personal beliefs, and uncertainty about one's rights, which may have contributed to this process.

People often fail to assert themselves in a particular situation because they previously have been punished either physically or verbally for expressing themselves in that situation. We have been punished by our parents, teachers, and other community members for behaving in certain ways. If you were punished as a child for expressing your opinions, particularly opinions which disagreed with others, you now may feel uncomfortable or uptight in situations which call for you to express youself. Feeling uptight or anxious is unpleasant for most of us and is something we seek to reduce or avoid. One way of reducing anxiety in the above situation is to not express our opinions—to behave nonassertively.

Perhaps you can recall one of your teachers or professors reprimanding you after you answered a question incorrectly or asked a question that the teacher felt was inappropriate. You may remember feeling upset by your teacher's scorn and embarrassed in the presence of your classmates. The anxiety caused by a few experiences such as this one may contribute to an inability to freely express yourself in other group meetings.

Similarly, you may remember refusing to help a friend straighten up the playroom because the friend had deliberately strewn all the toys across the room. Unfortunately, at that moment one of your parents, who had no knowledge of the situation, walked in and insisted you were misbehaving. You were made to straighten the room yourself and were also sent to your bedroom for the rest of the afternoon. In this situation, you were unjustly punished for refusing an unreasonable request. After a number of similar experiences, you quickly learned that it was better to give in to most requests than to suffer punishment for not doing so.

Thus one way that we learn not to express ourselves in a particular situation is by being punished repeatedly for expressing ourselves in that situation and thereby developing feelings of discomfort. We relieve these feelings of discomfort by not expressing ourselves. Unfortunately, this often results in the development of such habitual nonassertive responses as passive disagreement, silence, or pretending to agree by head nodding or expressing an opinion contrary to what we really believe.

A person also may learn to behave nonassertively in a situation because nonassertive behavior is rewarded or reinforced in that situation. A behavior that is rewarded or reinforced is more likely to reoccur in the future in the same situation. Thus if you behave nonassertively and others reward you for this behavior, you are quite likely to behave that way again. For instance, suppose a friend asks you to make a special trip downtown to pick up a package so that he/she won't be late to his/her weekly card game. To fulfill the request means considerable inconvenience for you at this time. If you behave nonassertively and comply, it is quite likely that your friend will praise you and say nice things to you. Even though you felt the request was untimely, the reinforcement from your friend increases the chances that you will continue to hide your real feelings and comply with his/her requests in the future.

In many instances, punishment of assertive behavior and reinforcement of nonassertive behavior occur at the same time. For example, research in the field of education has shown us that much of the interpersonal behavior that children learn in school involves being passive, silent, and not rocking the boat. The obedient, quiet child often tends to be valued and praised (reinforced) by teachers, whereas the inquisitive, opinion-giving child may be seen as disruptive or unruly and may be punished more often than his less assertive counterpart. Thus children often learn from formal education that it is better or perhaps safer to be seen and not heard.

The behavior generally displayed by significant individuals around us as we were growing up is another important influence on the development of nonassertive behavior. Much of what we learn occurs through a process called "modeling." Modeling involves observing and imitating behaviors of significant others around us. For example, if your parents rarely expressed feelings of affection openly, you also may have learned not to express feelings of affection. Similarly, if your parents usually gave in to the demands of others even though this caused considerable inconvenience, you may have learned to accommodate others while denying yourself. Perhaps you can recall your next-door neighbor Mr. Smith, who was always borrowing, but seldom returning, your father's prized power tools. Even though dad grumbled and complained about this when Mr. Smith wasn't around, he continued to lend his tools because he felt that it was so important to be a "good" neighbor. Are you now repeating the same pattern with your friends and neighbors?

A fourth contributing factor involves lack of opportunity to develop appropriate behavior. Many individuals behave nonassertively in social situations because they have not had the opportunity in the past to learn appropriate ways of behaving. When confronted by the new situation, they are at a loss for how to respond and in addition may feel uptight because of their lack of knowledge. For instance, the college freshman who is just beginning to date because previously his/her parents felt that the individual was too young for such activities may report feeling uptight because "I didn't know how to begin a conversation with my date," or "I couldn't make small talk, since I had never done that before." The individual reports that he/she was too passive because he/she did not know how to behave. Another example is provided by the individual who reports difficulty coping with sales persons because previously "my parents/spouse took care of those matters for me and I never had to pay much attention or worry about how to cope with situations in which I didn't like what the salesperson was showing me."

Another factor involves cultural standards and personal beliefs that serve as learned proscriptions against assertive behavior. Different cultural groups teach their members different ways to behave in social situations. For instance, one woman who presented herself for an assertion training group indicated that the cultural standards that she had learned as a child were counterproductive to her as an adult and as a professional. She reported that she had been raised in a Latin American country, where she had learned that women were supposed to be passive and not voice opinions. However, as an adult in the United States she found that she felt extremely tense and uptight because she was frequently required to voice opinions, particularly in her professional work. The cultural standards that she had learned as a child were in opposition to the behavior required in her personal and professional life as an adult and were causing substantial discomfort and confusion for her.

In addition to cultural standards, we also acquire a variety of personal beliefs that can interfere with the expression of assertive behavior. We learn and act on such beliefs as "If you can't say something nice about a person, don't say anything at all" or "I must be liked by everyone." Guiding one's behavior in rigid accordance with these and other beliefs often results in the inhibition of expression of one's feelings, attitudes, and opinions.

Finally, people often fail to behave assertively in a situation because they are unsure about their rights in that situation. They may never have learned what their rights are. If you are not sure of your rights and those of the other person, the likelihood that you will behave assertively in a situation is reduced significantly.

This manual is concerned with helping you to develop assertive behavior in situations where you previously have behaved nonassertively. In many ways the development of assertive behavior follows the same principles as that of nonassertive behavior. Thus in learning assertive behavior you will find that we will ask you to develop opportunities and situations that call for assertive behavior, and we will ask you to practice assertive behavior repeatedly and reward yourself for doing so. In addition, we will ask you to question cultural standards and beliefs that may be prohibiting you from behaving assertively in a particular situation.

EXERCISE MODULE 1
ASSESSING YOUR BEHAVIOR

In Discussion Module 1, you learned that assertive behavior involves directly expressing your feelings, preferences, needs, rights, and opinions without undue anxiety and in a manner that is neither threatening nor punishing to others. You also may recall that assertion consists of numerous behaviors directed toward various people. Individuals differ in their ability to express these behaviors and in their ability to interact effectively with these persons.

Before learning more about behaving assertively, it would be helpful to determine how you presently express yourself. As with other skill-training programs—such as speed reading—assertion training is enhanced if an assessment of the participant's skills is conducted prior to begininng the program. The assessment provides information that is helpful in tailoring the program to meet the specific needs of the individual user. The more closely your training program fits your needs, the more likely you are to derive maximum benefit from it.

In this module, an assessment procedure, the Assertion Self-Assessment Table, is presented to help you determine the specific behaviors and persons to focus on during your training program. It also will be valuable to use the self-assessment procedure periodically during the training program to evaluate your progress and to modify the training as needed.

Assertion Self-Assessment Table

Now turn to the Assertion Self-Assessment Table and detach it from the manual. Notice that the row headings list a variety of behaviors that represent the major categories of assertion: expression of positive feelings, expression of self-affirmation, and expression of negative feelings. The column headings list persons to whom these behaviors may be addressed. The persons represented are not inclusive of all people with whom you may interact. Some columns contain more than one person. In these instances, you should choose the person who is most relevant for you. For example, if you are married, you will be answering (in most cases) questions about your behavior with your spouse, rather than boyfriend/girlfriend. The darkened cells indicate situations that are unlikely to be relevant for most people. There may be other situations that are not applicable to you. Simply ignore those cells that do not apply.

The Assertion Self-Assessment Table will be used to evaluate frequency of assertions, presence of anxiety, and areas of aggression. By completing Steps 1-6, you will determine how frequently you assert ten different behaviors with eight different persons. Your responses to Steps 7-12 will indicate whether or not you experience undue anxiety while expressing yourself, and Steps 13-19 will help you evaluate whether you are aggressive while expressing particular behaviors with given persons.

Frequency of Asserting Yourself

Step 1. In reading the table, use the following question with each row and column heading:
Do I (*row heading*) to/from/of/with (*column heading*) when it is appropriate?
For instance, if you begin with the upper left hand cell, you would form the following question: Do I *give compliments* to *friends of the same sex* when it is appropriate?

Step 2. In answering the question for each cell, write in the word which best describes how often you engage in the behavior in that situation. Choose your answer from

Exercise Module 1

the words *usually, sometimes,* or *seldom.* For example, if you *seldom* give compliments to friends of the same sex when appropriate, you would write the word *seldom* in the upper left hand cell of the table.

Step 3. Now complete each cell in the table in the manner described in Steps 1 and 2.

Step 4. Look at the table and find the places where you answered with the words *seldom* and *sometimes.* Are there one or more behaviors (for example, making requests) for which you have given a number of *seldom* and *sometimes* answers? If there are, list those behaviors here.

_____
_____
_____
_____

    We suggest that you devote special attention to these behaviors when you design your assertion training program. Discussion and Exercise Modules 5-13 provide information and exercises to help you with these behaviors. Each of these discussion and exercise modules has been designed to deal with one of the behaviors in the assessment. If you glance at the table of contents, you can quickly locate the particular modules that will be most relevant to you based on the results of your self-assessment.

Step 5. Again, look at the places where you have the words *seldom* and *sometimes.* Are there one or more persons (for example, intimate relations: spouses, boyfriends, girlfriends) for whom you have a given number of *seldom* and *sometimes* answers? If there are, list those persons here.

_____
_____
_____
_____

    We suggest that you devote special attention to these persons when you design your assertion training program. Exercise Modules 14-18 are concerned with assertion with special persons and in special situations. In particular, discussion and exercise modules have been prepared to help you with assertion with the following persons: parents and other family members, authority figures, spouses and other intimate relations (couples), and co-workers, colleagues and subordinates (work situations).

Step 6. As you look at your *seldom* and *sometimes* answers, you may find that they do not group into any particular behaviors or persons. This is not uncommon, since people often have difficulty expressing only certain feelings to only certain people. Under these circumstances, you will have to select the most relevant discussion and exercise modules from the manual when you design your assertion training program.

TABLE 1
Assertion Self-Assessment Table

Behaviors	Friends of the same sex	Friends of the opposite sex	Intimate relations, e.g. spouse, boyfriend, girlfriend,	Parents, in-laws, and other family members	Children	Authority figures, e.g. bosses, professors, doctors	Business contacts, e.g. salespersons, waiters	Co-workers colleagues, and subordinates
Expressing Positive Feelings <u>Give compliments</u>								
Receive compliments								
Make requests, e.g. ask for favors, help, etc.								
Express liking, love, and affection								
Initiate and maintain conversations								
Self-Affirmation <u>Stand up for your legitimate rights</u>								
Refuse requests								
Express personal opinions including disagreement								
Expressing Negative Feelings <u>Express justified annoyance and displeasure</u>								
Express justified anger								

Persons

Presence of Anxiety

Step 7. To assess whether you experience any discomfort or undue anxiety when you express yourself, use the following question with each row and column heading:
When I (*row heading*) to/from/of/with (*column heading*), do I become very nervous or unduly anxious?
For instance, if you begin with the upper left hand cell, you would form the following question: When I *give compliments* to *friends of the same sex*, do I become very nervous or unduly anxious?

Step 8. For each cell, answer the question with either a *yes* or *no*. If you answer *yes*, write *yes* in the cell. For example, if you become very nervous when you compliment a friend of the same sex, write *yes* in the upper left-hand cell. If you answer *no*, leave the cell blank.

Step 9. Now complete each cell in the table in the manner described in Steps 7 and 8.

Step 10. Look at the table and note where you entered the word *yes*. Are there particular behaviors for which you have given a number of *yes* responses? If there are, list those behaviors here.

_____
_____
_____
_____

If you choose to include these behaviors in your assertion training program, you may want to incorporate relaxation training, which is described in Exercise Module 4.

Step 11. Again, look at your *yes* answers. Are there particular persons for whom you have given a number of *yes* responses? If there are, list those persons here.

_____
_____
_____
_____

If you choose to include situations dealing with these persons in your assertion training program, you also may want to incorporate the relaxation training which is described in Exercise Module 4.

Step 12. Some of you may find that your *yes* answers do not group under any particular behaviors or persons. This is not uncommon, since people often experience anxiety only when expressing certain feelings to certain people.

Exercise Module 1

Evaluation of Aggressive Behavior

Step 13. If you are considering assertion training because you feel that your behavior is aggressive at times, continue with Steps 14-19. If this is not a concern of yours, skip over these steps and read the concluding remarks of this module.

Step 14. As you may know, aggression may be direct and include such behaviors as threats, hostile remarks, name calling, and ridicule, or it may be indirect and include such behaviors as sarcasm and malicious gossip. To determine whether you behave aggressively at times, use the following question with each row and column heading:

   Am I aggressive when I (*row heading*) to/from/of/with (*column heading*)?

For instance, if you are reading the lower right-hand cell (last cell in table), you would form the following question: Am I aggressive when I *express justified anger* to *co-workers?*

Step 15. In answering the question for each cell, *shade* in those cells for which you report behaving aggressively in that situation.

Step 16. Complete each cell in the table in the manner described in Steps 14 and 15.

Step 17. Look at the table and note the cells you have shaded. Are there one or more behaviors for which you have shaded a number of cells? If there are, list those behaviors here.

_____
_____
_____
_____

We suggest that you devote special attention to these behaviors when you design your assertion training program. In particular, Discussion and Exercise Modules 2 present material on recognizing and discriminating assertive, aggressive, and nonassertive ways of responding in a situation.

Step 18. Again, note the cells you have shaded. Are there particular persons for whom you have shaded a number of cells? If there are, list those persons here.

_____
_____
_____
_____

We suggest that you devote special attention to these persons when you design your assertion training program.

Step 19. You may find that your shaded cells do not group under any particular behaviors or persons. This is not uncommon, since people often are aggressive only when expressing certain behaviors to certain people.

Concluding Remarks

We hope this personal assessment has increased your awareness and helped you to decide whether you would like to change any of your behaviors with any particular persons. Regardless of the results of your self-asesssment, there is no reason for you to change your behavior if you are satisfied with it. Assertion training is not for everyone. However, if you would like to feel comfortable and be more effective in expressing yourself, assertion training can be quite helpful.

Now that you have completed your self-assessment, continue reading Chapter One. At the end of the chapter, instructions on using the results of your self-assessment in planning your assertion training program are provided.

Discussion Module **2**

Recognizing Nonassertive, Aggressive, and Assertive Behavior

In order to behave assertively in a situation, you first need to understand what constitutes assertive behavior. An effective way to develop this understanding is by contrasting assertive behavior with aggressive and nonassertive ways of responding. This procedure was suggested by R.E. Alberti and M.L. Emmons, *Your Perfect Right: A Guide to Assertive Behavior.*

Nonassertive Behavior

When a person behaves nonassertively in a situation, he/she may fail to express his/her feelings, needs, opinions, or preferences, or he/she may express them in an indirect or implicit manner. For example, verbally agreeing to activities one really is not interested in or failing to ask a favor even though one is needed represent the denial of one's opinions and needs. Accompanying the verbal denial may be such nonassertive nonverbal behaviors as avoidance of eye contact, hesitant speech pattern, low voice level, tense body posture, and nervous or inappropriate body movements.

Statements such as "I suppose we could go to the movies" or "I wish I knew someone who could teach me to jack up my car" represent indirect or implicit verbal communications in which the other party must infer what the needs or opinions of the speaker really are. One difficulty with indirect, incomplete, or implicit communication is that it is open to varying interpretations and therefore is easily misunderstood. The reason it can be misunderstood is that mixed messages are being delivered. In some cases, the person's verbal and nonverbal behaviors are inconsistent or contradictory in the message. The person verbalizes that he/she would be delighted to do this favor but is frowning at the same time. In other instances, the verbal message itself is inconsistent; for example, "Andre's sounds fine for dinner. Do you know anyone who has enjoyed the food there that much?"

Behaving nonassertively in a situation means denying or restricting your rights because you fail to express how you feel or you express it in an indirect way. Also, when you behave nonassertively, you place the responsibility for making decisions that affect everyone in the situation solely on the other person(s).

Behaving nonassertively in a situation can result in a number of undesirable consequences for both the person who is behaving nonassertively and for the individual with whom he/she is interacting. The likelihood that the person who is behaving nonassertively will have his/her needs satisfied or that his/her opinions will be understood is substantially reduced due to the lack of communication or to indirect or incomplete communication. The person who behaves nonassertively often will feel misunderstood, taken for granted, and used. In addition, he/she may feel angry about the outcome of the situation or become hostile or annoyed toward the other person. He/she may feel badly about himself/herself as a result of being unable to adequately express his/her opinions or feelings. This can lead to feelings of guilt, depression, anxiety, and lowered self-esteem. People who characteristically behave nonassertively across a variety of situations may develop such psychosomatic complaints as headaches and ulcers due to the suppression of pent-up feelings. Further, after numerous situations in which an individual has been nonassertive, he/she may find himself/herself blowing up. There is a limit to how much frustration an individual can bottle up inside himself/herself. Unfortunately, at this juncture, the amount of annoyance or anger that is expressed is often out of proportion to the present precipitating situation.

The recipient of nonassertive behavior also may experience a variety of unfavorable consequences. Having to infer constantly what the other person is "really saying" or having to "read the other person's mind" is a difficult and taxing endeavor which can lead to feelings of frustration or to annoyance or anger toward the person who is behaving nonassertively. Worrying or feeling guilty about whether you are taking advantage of the person who is not really saying what he/she means is unpleasant and can result in weakening whatever positive feelings you have for that person. Finally, it is a heavy burden to have the responsibility of making decisions for another person and then to find that he/she may not be satisfied with the choices that you have made.

Aggressive Behavior

In aggressive behavior, the individual expresses his/her feelings and opinions but does so in a punishing, threatening, assaultive, demanding, or hostile manner. The person who engages in aggressive behavior in a situation disregards or infringes on the other person's rights. Thus in aggressive behavior there is little or no consideration of the feelings and rights of the person who is the object of the aggression. In addition, the person who behaves aggressively in the situation assumes little responsibility for the consequences of his/her action.

Aggressive behavior in a situation can be expressed in either a direct or indirect manner. Direct verbal aggression includes verbal assaults, name calling, threats, and humiliating and hostile remarks. The nonverbal component may include hostile or threatening gestures, such as fist waving and glaring looks, and physical assaults. The following are examples of some verbally aggressive statements:

You'd *better* lend me $5.
You are a no good S.O.B.
You are *going* with me whether you like it or not.

Indirect verbal aggression includes sarcastic remarks, catty comments, and malicious gossip. Indirect nonverbal aggressive behaviors include physical gestures performed while the person's attention is directed elsewhere, or physical acts directed toward other persons or objects. The following are examples of indirect aggression.

Sarcasm. A colleague has given you the final draft of his/her half of the report that you've both been working on for some time now. You read it and feel it needs a lot more work. Rather than tell him/her directly, you sarcastically say, "Hey, Joe/Jane, you know that report you gave me? Not bad for a *rough* draft."

Malicious Gossip. You're quite annoyed at your neighbor because you told him/her about a month ago you were planning to have a party on the Fourth of July. After all your plans were made except for the invitations, you received an invitation from him/her for the same night. Instead of confronting him/her, you begin telling neighbors that he/she stole your ideas; that they shouldn't go to his/her party since he/she will just exploit them; that you can't trust him/her; that he/she is having this party since he/she and his/her spouse are having difficulties and he/she wants to impress the spouse.

The major characteristic of aggressive behavior is the achievement of one's goals in a situation with little regard for and at the expense of the other individual(s). Aggressive behavior often is regarded as pushy behavior, since one attempts to achieve goals at any expense, pushing aside people and other obstacles in the process.

Aggressive behavior often results in unfavorable consequences for both the aggressor and the object of the aggression. The unfavorable effects of aggressive behavior on the recipient are obvious. His/her rights have been denied. He/she may feel humiliated, embarrassed, or abused. In addition, the recipient may feel resentful or angry and seek revenge through direct or indirect means.

Although the person who behaves aggressively in a situation may achieve desired goals, he/she may experience unfavorable consequences both immediately and in the future. Aggressive behavior often results in immediate and more forceful direct counteraggression in the form of physical or verbal abuse. Aggression may also lead to indirect counteraggression in the form of a softly delivered sarcastic retort or a defiant glance. Long-range consequences may include strain in the interpersonal relationship with the other person or avoidance of further contact by the other person. After behaving aggressively, the individual may suffer feelings of guilt and remorse for his/her behavior. However, since he/she has achieved desired goals (been reinforced) through aggressive behavior, it is likely that he/she will continue to behave aggressively in that situation in the future and simply tolerate the subsequent guilt feelings that may arise, unless the latter are exceedingly strong.

Assertive Behavior

Assertive behavior involves the direct expression of one's feelings, needs, legitimate rights, or opinions without being punishing or threatening to others and without infringing upon their rights. In addition, assertive behavior does not involve an excessive or undue amount of fear or anxiety. One's nonverbal behavior, such as eye contact, facial expression, body posture, and tone and loudness of voice, are also quite important and may add or detract from the verbal behavior. These behaviors need to be harmonious with the verbal content of the assertive message. For instance, when one is expressing feelings of affection, the tone and loudness of voice are quite different from when one expresses annoyance or displeasure. A further discussion of these nonverbal behaviors is presented in Discussion Module 3.

In contrast to nonassertive behavior, assertive behavior involves expressing one's feelings and opinions honestly and directly rather than hoping that the other person will read one's mind. For instance, rather than nonassertively saying to your neighbor, "Do you have any eggs in the house?" you might say, "Do you have two eggs I could borrow for the cake I'm planning to make tonight?" In the nonassertive remark, your neighbor does not know you want to borrow two eggs. In fact, he/she may think you have extra eggs you want to give him/her. In the assertive statement, you clearly state that you would like to borrow two eggs. It would be unlikely that your neighbor could misinterpret this direct request. It is important to stress that whether your neighbor has two eggs or one thousand eggs, he/she is under no obligation to let you borrow the eggs regardless of the manner in which you make your request. Your only responsibility is to ask in an assertive fashion so that your request is clear, and to respect the other person's reply. Depending on your neighbor's reply, you may or may not need to repeat your request. If your neighbor gives you a definitive reply, such as, "Sure, Sam/Sue, here are two eggs," or "Sorry, Sam/Sue, I can't spare the two eggs tonight," then you need to respect his/her wishes. However, if your neighbor replies, "Well, how many do you need?" or "Do you have to have them tonight?" you need to answer his/her question and repeat your request if necessary. Multiple requests seem appropriate if a clear answer is not received. Judgments need to be made continuously concerning what is appropriate and assertive for a particular situation.

An aggressive approach to the egg-borrowing situation might involve a demand for the two eggs or repeated demands after a definitive answer has been given. In addition, the demand for the eggs may be coupled with sarcastic or derogatory comments and hostile gestures. For example:

Person 1: Hey, *give* me two of your eggs. I'm baking a cake tonight.
Person 2: Well, I'm really running low on them and I need them for some baking that I'm doing. I really can't spare them.
Person 1: Look, don't be so difficult. Just give me the two crummy eggs.

In this situation, it appears that Person 1 is attempting to force or to make Person 2 responsible for the satisfaction of his/her needs. The behavior displayed by Person 1 is an attempt to deny the rights of Person 2 in this situation.

Assertive behavior is not designed primarily to enable an individaul to obtain what he/she wants. Rather, its purpose is the clear, direct, and inoffensive communication of one's needs, opinions, and so on. To the extent that this is accomplished, the probability of achieving one's goals without denying the rights of others is increased.

Assertive behavior is expressed with consideration of rights, responsibilities, and consequences. The person expressing himself/herself in a situation needs to consider what his/her rights are in that situation and what the rights are of the others involved. The individual also needs to be cognizant of his/her responsibilities in that situation and the consequences resulting from the expression of his/her feelings. For instance, if a friend has both failed to meet you for an arranged meeting and failed to call to break the engagement, you have a right to express how you feel, but you also need to determine if there were extenuating circumstances. You have a responsibility to listen to your friend's response in case the situation was unavoidable (someone suddenly got sick, the car broke down in an out-of-the-way area, or so on). You will want to express how you feel, keeping in mind the consequences of your statements. For instance, if your friend just forgot or decided to go elsewhere, you need to consider the consequences of expressing your annoyance. In the short run, your friend will feel slightly upset, but in the long run he/she will be less likely to repeat this behavior, thereby increasing the likelihood of a more satisfactory relationship between the two or you.

Does assertive behavior in a situation always result in the absence of conflict between two

Discussion Module 2

parties? No. The total absence of conflict between two parties is an impossibility. There are certain situations in which assertive behavior is appropriate and desirable but may cause some annoyance to the other person. For example, returning a defective piece of merchandise to a harried store clerk in an assertive—or perhaps in any other—manner may not be welcomed warmly. Similarly, expressing justified annoyance or legitimate criticism in an appropriate manner may bring an initial unfavorable reaction. Weighing the short-term and long-term consequences for both parties is what is important. It seems to us that assertive behavior results in maximizing favorable consequences and minimizing unfavorable consequences for individuals over the long run.

Assertive behavior in a situation *generally* results in favorable consequences to the parties that are involved. The person who has asserted himself/herself may or may not accomplish his/her objectives, but he/she generally feels better about having been able to state his/her opinions. The clear statement of one's position is likely to enhance the probability that the other person will respect that position and then behave accordingly. Thus, people who behave assertively in a situation express their rights, make their own choices and decisions, and accept responsibility for their behavior.

Favorable consequences also are likely to occur for the person who is the object of assertive behavior in a situation. This person receives a clear and nonmanipulative communication, in contrast to the unstated or implied communication that is transmitted in nonassertive behavior. In addition, he/she receives a request for new behavior or a statement of the other person's position rather than the demand for new behavior that is characteristic of aggression. As a result, there are few chances for misinterpretation. Although the other person may not agree, accept, or like what the assertive behavior relates (I love you; I like your dress; I'm annoyed that you forgot to call me as you said you would; I prefer not to let you drive my car), the manner in which it is delivered does not deny his/her rights, does not put him/her down, and does not force him/her to make another's decision or to take responsibility for someone else's behavior.

What happens when both parties behave assertively in a situation? This is probably a very desirable state of affairs. If the positions or opinions of the two parties are compatible, then both will be satisfied by the interaction. If the positions are incompatible, then both parties can clearly recognize this and attempt to compromise or negotiate if they so choose or simply respect each other's right to disagree and not attempt to impose demands on each other. In the latter case, each can feel satisfied that he/she has expressed himself/herself while recognizing and accepting that his/her goal may not have been achieved.

EXERCISE MODULE 2
DISCRIMINATING NONASSERTIVE, AGGRESSIVE, AND ASSERTIVE BEHAVIOR

Now that you have read Discussion Module 2 concerning the differences between **nonassertive, aggressive, and assertive behavior,** it is time for you to begin putting this knowledge to work. A number of situations will be described below. For each situation, three different responses will follow. You are to mark each response as nonassertive, aggressive, or assertive. An evaluation of each answer appears at the top of the next page. Be sure to check your responses. If you find that you are having difficulty with this exercise, go back and reread Discussion Module 2.

The tone of voice, inflections, and nonverbal behaviors have not been included in this exercise. However, keep in mind that nonverbal behavior and tone of voice play an important role in self-expression.

Situation 1

Your friend has just arrived an hour late for dinner. He/she did not call to let you know that he/she would be detained. You are annoyed about his/her lateness. You say:

1a. Come on in. Dinner's on the table.
☐ assertive
☐ nonassertive
☐ aggressive

1b. I've been waiting for an hour. I would have appreciated your calling to let me know you would be late.
☐ assertive
☐ nonassertive
☐ aggressive

1c. You've got a lot of nerve coming late. That's the last time I'll invite you.
☐ assertive
☐ nonassertive
☐ aggressive

Responses to Situation 1

1a. Nonassertive, because you pretend that nothing has happened. You neither mention that your friend is late nor that you are displeased by his/her behavior.
1b. Assertive, because you tell your friend that he/she is late, that you have been waiting, and that you feel he/she should have called.
1c. Aggressive, because you put your friend down (you've got a lot of nerve) and threaten him (won't invite you again).

Situation 2

Your parents have just criticized your spouse/boyfriend/girlfriend. You feel the criticism is unjustified. You say:

2a. Shut up. You're both so stupid and prejudiced.
☐ assertive
☐ nonassertive
☐ aggressive

2b. Well, I see what you mean.
☐ assertive
☐ nonassertive
☐ aggressive

2c. I feel your criticism is unfair. He/she is not like that at all.
☐ assertive
☐ nonassertive
☐ aggressive

chapter 1: Fundamentals of Assertion

Responses to Situation 2

2a. Aggressive, because you behave hostilely toward your parents and you call them a name (stupid).
2b. Nonassertive, because you don't agree with what your parents said, but you imply you do (I see what you mean).
2c. Assertive, because you express how you feel (I feel your criticism is unfair).

Situation 3

A friend has just complimented you on your new suit. It's the first time you've worn it and you really like it. You say:

3a. Thank you.
    ☐ assertive
    ☐ nonassertive
    ☐ aggressive

3b. This? It's nothing special.
    ☐ assertive
    ☐ nonassertive
    ☐ aggressive

3c. Well . . . I picked it up at a sale . . . well. . . .
    ☐ assertive
    ☐ nonassertive
    ☐ aggressive

Exercise Module 2

Responses to Situation 3

- 3a. Assertive, because you accept and acknowledge the compliment.
- 3b. Nonassertive, because you do not accept the compliment. You say it's nothing special, although you know it's the first time you've worn it, and you really do like it.
- 3c. Nonassertive, because you do not accept the compliment.

Situation 4

You're out with a group of friends. You're all deciding which movie to see. One person has just mentioned a movie you don't want to see. You say:

- 4a. You always pick movies I don't like. You only think about yourself. You're very selfish.
  - ☐ assertive
  - ☐ nonassertive
  - ☐ aggressive

- 4b. I don't want to see that one. How about a movie over at the Plaza Theatre?
  - ☐ assertive
  - ☐ nonassertive
  - ☐ aggressive

- 4c. Well, I don't know much about that movie. But, I guess, if you want to, we can see it.
  - ☐ assertive
  - ☐ nonassertive
  - ☐ aggressive

Responses to Situation 4

4a. Aggressive, because you attack your friend (you're very selfish) rather than saying, "I don't want to see that one" and then suggesting another one.

4b. Assertive, because you express your opinion (I don't want to see that one) and make another suggestion.

4c. Nonassertive, because you don't express your opinion. You say, "If you want to, we can see it," but you don't really want to see it.

Situation 5

You are returning a faulty item to the department store. You bought a shirt/blouse. When you took it home, you found a misweave in it. You do not want the item as it is. The clerk has just said no one will ever notice it. You say:

5a. Well, I'd still like to return it or exchange it. I do not want this one.
☐ assertive
☐ nonassertive
☐ aggressive

5b. Look, give me my money. I don't have all day for you to waste my time.
☐ assertive
☐ nonassertive
☐ aggressive

5c. Well, are you sure no one will notice it?
☐ assertive
☐ nonassertive
☐ aggressive

Exercise Module 2

Responses to Situation 5

5a. Assertive, because you tell the clerk exactly what you want. While acknowledging his point of view, you still want to return or exchange the shirt.
5b. Aggressive, because you accuse the clerk of wasting your time.
5c. Nonassertive, because you do not want this faulty merchandise.

Situation 6

You love your spouse/boyfriend/girlfriend very much and want to express this feeling to him/her. You've just finished a quiet dinner in your home and are sitting alone. You say:

6a. I enjoyed the dinner. Oh . . . well . . . how do you feel?
☐ assertive
☐ nonassertive
☐ aggressive

6b. Dear, I really love you. You're great.
☐ assertive
☐ nonassertive
☐ aggressive

6c. Well, what's new?
☐ assertive
☐ nonassertive
☐ aggressive

Responses to Situation 6

6a. Nonassertive, because you do not express how you feel. You talk about dinner rather than your feelings of affection.
6b. Assertive, because you state how you feel.
6c. Nonassertive, because you do not express what you want to say. You engage in small talk when you really want to express your affection.

Situation 7

Your parents have just called and said they are coming to visit tonight. You already have plans for the evening that you do not want to break. You say:

7a. Mom, I've seen you twice this week. Enough is enough. You are always bugging me. You're a pain.
☐ assertive
☐ nonassertive
☐ aggressive

7b. Sure, I'd be glad to see you tonight, but couldn't you come tomorrow?
☐ assertive
☐ nonassertive
☐ aggressive

7c. Mom, not tonight. I already have plans for the evening.
☐ assertive
☐ nonassertive
☐ aggressive

Exercise Module 2

Responses to Situation 7

7a. Aggressive, because you put your mother down. You tell her she's a pain and she bugs you. You never tell her that you already have plans for this evening so she can't come.

7b. Nonassertive, because you only imply that perhaps tomorrow would be better while at the same time saying you'd be glad to see her tonight. The point is you already have plans tonight. You have given her a double message.

7c. Assertive, because you tell your mom you have a previous engagement and therefore can't see her tonight.

Situation 8

You'd like your child to go down the block and pick up a package at your friend's house. You say:

8a. Billy, I'd like it if you would go over to Mrs. Smith's and pick up a package for me. I'd appreciate it if you could do it by 3 o'clock.
☐ assertive
☐ nonassertive
☐ aggressive

8b. If you aren't too busy, well . . . will you be going by Mrs. Smith's today?
☐ assertive
☐ nonassertive
☐ aggressive

8c. Hey, it's about time you did something worthwhile. Go down to Mrs. Smith's and pick up a package for me. No back talk. Stop being such a lazy thing. Go on.
☐ assertive
☐ nonassertive
☐ aggressive

Responses to Situation 8

8a. Assertive, because you ask your child directly to do a favor for you. You neither demand nor threaten him/her. Your request is stated in such a manner that he/she is free to respond to it.
8b. Nonassertive, because you never ask your child to pick up the package. You never come to the point.
8c. Aggressive, because you demand rather than ask your child to do a favor for you. You also insult him.

Situation 9

A co-worker keeps giving you all of his/her work to do. You've decided to put an end to this. Your co-worker has just asked you to do some more of his/her work. You say:

9a. I'm kind of busy. But if you can't get it done, I guess I can help you.
☐ assertive
☐ nonassertive
☐ aggressive

9b. Forget it. It's about time you do it. You treat me like your slave. You're an inconsiderate S.O.B.
☐ assertive
☐ nonassertive
☐ aggressive

9c. No, Sue/Tom, I'm not going to do any more of your work. I'm tired of doing both my work and your work.
☐ assertive
☐ nonassertive
☐ aggressive

Responses to Situation 9

9a. Nonassertive, because you do not tell your co-worker you're tired of doing his/her work. You agree to help even though you do not want to.
9b. Aggressive, because you make accusations and engage in name calling.
9c. Assertive, because you express how you feel (I'm tired of doing your work) and what you plan to do (I'm not going to do your work any more).

Situation 10

A new person/family has just moved in next door. You really want to meet him/her/them.

10a. You smile as your neighbor(s) walk by, but say nothing.
☐ assertive
☐ nonassertive
☐ aggressive

10b. You go next door and say, "Hi. I'm Sue/Tom. I live next door. Welcome to the neighborhood. I'm glad to meet you."
☐ assertive
☐ nonassertive
☐ aggressive

10c. You watch your neighbor through your window.
☐ assertive
☐ nonassertive
☐ aggressive

Responses to Situation 10

10a. Assertive/nonassertive. This response gets two ratings because the nonverbal behavior is assertive. You smile to your neighbor to show your interest, but your verbal behavior is nonassertive; you don't say anything. You need to introduce yourself to your neighbor if you want to meet him/her/them.
10b. Assertive, because you go and introduce yourself.
10c. Nonassertive, because you will not meet your neighbor(s) by just watching.

Reminder: If you had difficulty marking the responses to these ten situations, reread Discussion Module 2 before proceeding to Discussion Module 3.

Discussion Module **3**

Assertion Training Procedures and Criteria of Assertive Behavior

This module discusses the procedures that you will use in your assertion training program. Since people learn in different ways, a variety of training procedures are presented. In your program, you may need to emphasize certain of these steps and procedures and de-emphasize others. The point is to use the procedures that are most helpful to you. We suggest that you begin by following our basic sequence and then tailor the procedures to your unique requirements. What is important is the *repeated* and *systematic* use of these training procedures.

The purpose of any assertion training program is to help you develop assertive responses in those situations in which you would like to improve your behavior. You may recognize that you do not behave assertively in certain situations but decide that you do not want to change your behavior. In these instances you would exclude the situations from your training program.

Now look at your answers to the Assertion Self-Assessment Table. Consult the list of cells in which you reported that you seldom assert yourself, that you experience undue anxiety, and that you behave aggressively. Arrange the behaviors and persons in these lists in order of difficulty, from those in which it will be easiest to modify your behavior to those in which it will be most difficult. We suggest you begin your training program with the easiest situations and then progress to the more difficult ones as you develop skills and confidence. After you complete the remainder of this chapter, turn to the modules on the behavior you feel will be easiest to change. First read the discussion module on rights, responsibilities, and rationale for that behavior. Then complete the situations provided in the corresponding exercise modules. Each of these situations requires that you reply to an individual who says some standard lines to you in a conversation format.

Described below are the procedures used in assertion training. Following self-assessment, there are four main phases in learning to behave assertively. First you will appraise the situation with which you are presented in order to determine what assertive behavior is required. Second, you will practice the assertive behavior which is required in the situations through such means as writing your responses or role playing with another person. Then you will evaluate your behavior and repeat the situation until you are satisfied with your performance. The final phase consists of transferring your assertive behavior into your daily interactions.

Appraise the Situation

1. Determine what you believe the rights and responsibilities are of the various parties in the situation

In some instances, the rights and responsibilities of the parties are clear and understood by all concerned, whereas in other situations they are either unclear or are not shared by everyone. In the former situations, those behaviors which are appropriate and assertive are clear, whereas in the latter they may not be. Thus rights and responsibilities are important in determining what behaviors are appropriate and assertive in a given situation.

What are your rights and responsibilities? It is impossible to answer this question satisfactorily. Rights and responsibilities vary with the person with whom one is interacting, the situation, the culture or ethnic group, and so on. To our knowledge, no universal doctrine of rights and responsibilities exists that is shared by everyone and that can be consulted as a guide to behavior in each and every situation.

In general, we feel that people have the *right* to express how they feel, what they believe, and so on, in an assertive manner. We also feel that they have the *responsibility* to listen to what the other person is saying and to respect a clear, definitive, and final reply by the other person. In Discussion Modules 5-18 we discuss what we believe are the general rights and responsibilities involved in asserting yourself. These rights and responsibilities may be used as guidelines to determine what behavior is appropriate in a situation. However, these guidelines are not designed to substitute for your considered judgment of what the social rights and responsibilities are in a given situation.

2. Determine the probable short-term and long-term consequences of various courses of action

Many behaviors have both short-term and long-term consequences. The ability to identify or predict these consequences is important. Nonassertive behavior in a situation often results in minimizing the probability of short-term unfavorable consequences to the individual but increases the probability of long-term unfavorable consequences. For example, a member of one of our groups complained that a friend was always borrowing money but never paying it back. The friendship seemed to have been strained as a result. An examination of the group member's behavior indicated that he reluctantly gave the money because he did not want his friend to be angry at him. At the same time, he found that he tended to avoid the friend in order not to lend him more money. He also was less patient with his friend on other matters. In the short run, nonassertive behavior resulted in avoiding some immediate unpleasantness; but a long-term strain in the relationship resulted. In contrast, an assertive remark such as the following may have resulted in an immediate confrontation without the long-term adverse effects on the relationship: "Joe, I don't like you constantly borrowing money from me, and I would appreciate your paying me back before I lend you any more."

We believe that assertion generally results in favorable consequences. However, other people can and do respond negatively to assertive behavior on occasion. Unfavorable reactions probably are more likely when you express negative feelings or self-affirmation than when you express positive feelings. We discuss the subject of possible adverse reactions to assertive behavior at greater length in the discussion modules of Chapter Three, Self-Affirmation, and Chapter Four, Expressing Negative Feelings. For the moment, we would like to mention that adverse reactions from people that you feel close to can be minimized when you begin your assertion training if you inform these individuals that you are trying to learn new ways of behaving and that you would appreciate their help and patience.

Without belaboring the point, it is important to determine the likely consequences of various courses of action and how you feel about each before you decide how you will behave.

3. Decide how you will behave in the situation

We feel that it is important for people to *choose* how they wish to behave and then to be responsible for that behavior. If one behaves assertively in a situation, one should behave this way as a result of a considered choice to do so. Similarly, if one is not assertive in a situation, it should be the result of a considered decision to behave in this manner rather than because of the lack of skills to behave otherwise.

Although we believe that it is important to appraise situations and to make considered choices before acting, we realize that this process takes time and that everyday interactions call for moment-to-moment decisions. What we are advocating is not an in-depth philosophical examination of one's motives and the meaning of life. Such an examination would result in a paralysis of action. Rather, we are suggesting that you do not blurt out the first thing that comes to mind but pause a second or two to make a quick—but not hasty—decision about how you choose to behave in the situation. We believe that with practice this process can occur very quickly in your day-to-day interactions.

Experiment with New Behaviors and Attitudes in Practice Situations

1. Try out your new behavior in the situations provided

To develop new habits, you must practice your new ways of responding until they become a natural part of you. Learning to behave assertively in a situation is just like learning to swim, to drive a car, or any other skill. It requires repeated practice. At first, it might seem awkward and unnatural because you have to pay attention to everything you say and do just as when you were learning to drive. As you practice, it will become more and more automatic and natural. We believe that practice, accompanied by evaluation, is probably the most important part of assertion training for the majority of people.

There are many ways to use the situations provided in Exercise Modules 5-18. We suggest that you begin with situations that are easy for you and then proceed to more difficult situations.

One way to use the situations is to read each standard line and then respond to it either in writing or aloud, keeping in mind the criteria described below in the section on evaluating your behavior. Then repeat each situation several times until your skills and confidence increase.

A second way to use the situations is to record the standard lines on audio tape. Then play the tape, stopping it after each line is delivered so that *you* can give your response.

Another way to use the situations is to role play them. Ask another person to repeat the standard lines to you in a conversation format. Practice responding assertively to each standard line as it is delivered. As you become more comfortable with the situation, the other person can alter the lines. This will allow you to practice coping with possible variations in the situation and will provide opportunities to make spontaneous responses. If you have a tape recorder, you may want to record the interaction so that you can play it back for evaluation.

Finally, if you have access to videotape equipment, you can record your interactions for later playback and evaluation. In using any type of record/playback equipment, it is important to realize that such equipment presents information to you in a manner to which you are not accustomed. Most of us have few opportunities to see or hear ourselves as others do. On the occasions when people have access to this type of information, some find that they are dissatisfied with how they look or sound. It is important to concentrate on what you actually are saying and doing rather than to be concerned that you do not appear and sound as you expected. Try to determine what you are doing well. Then pick one or two behaviors that you would like to improve. Remember that you need to practice each situation *repeatedly*, until you feel very comfortable with your behavior and feel satisfied that you have responded assertively.

2. Write your own situations to practice

We have provided a variety of situations that will allow you to practice assertive behavior. In some instances you will find that a situation may need to be modified to fit your particular circumstances. In other instances you may want to develop your own situations.

To be maximally effective, an assertion training program should be tailored to the unique needs of each individual. Writing your own situations is one way in which this can be accomplished. Each situation should contain two elements: a written description in which it is clear that assertive behavior is appropriate, and several lines to which you can reply. We recommend that you include several lines rather than only one since most social interactions involve a series of statements and responses between two persons. Also, if you practice asserting yourself several times rather than only once in a practice situation, it is likely that you will be better prepared to cope with everyday interactions, which usually are more difficult than practice situations.

You should rehearse your own situations in the same way as you rehearse the situations we have provided. Rehearse each situation several times. As you develop confidence, vary the lines of the other person. Evaluate each performance using the assertion training criteria which are discussed later in this module.

3. Dispute erroneous beliefs and counterproductive attitudes and replace them with more accurate and productive beliefs*

As you repeatedly rehearse a particular situation, you may find that your behavior does not improve. Something seems to interfere with your performance in the situation, but you have difficulty identifying what it is. At times people fail to assert themselves not because they lack the skills but because they act on erroneous beliefs that a particular assertion is inappropriate in a particular situation. As a result of subscribing to erroneous beliefs or counterproductive

---

*The importance of changing irrational beliefs has been stressed by A. Ellis, *Reason and Emotion in Psychotherapy*, New York: Lyle Stuart, 1962; and M.C. Maultsby, *Help Yourself to Happiness through Rational Self-Counseling*, Boston: Herman Publishing, Inc., 1975.

attitudes, they either fail to act in a situation or they take action that really is not in their best interests.

How do you know when you are acting on misconceptions or counterproductive attitudes? There are a number of cues that suggest that this might be occurring. First, if you are rehearsing a particular situation and you do not feel more comfortable after successive rehearsals, then you need to step back and determine what is occurring. Are you becoming more anxious because you are attempting to engage in behaviors which are in opposition to your values or beliefs? If so, are those values and beliefs erroneous or counterproductive?

Perhaps you are rehearsing a situation and you know what you would like to say, but your speech is hesitant and faltering. This is another cue for you to examine your beliefs to determine whether they are erroneous or counterproductive.

In another situation, you find yourself becoming increasingly aggressive or hostile. Once again, this is a signal that you need to think about what your beliefs are in the situation that may be influencing you to act in this aggressive manner.

Finally, you encounter one of the situations in the exercise modules or in your daily interactions, and your immediate response is, "I can't cope with this situation, even though I know it is appropriate to act assertively." This is another cue to examine your beliefs and attitudes.

As we have said previously, people develop a variety of beliefs and attitudes throughout their lives. Some of these are beneficial and adaptive, while some are not. Other beliefs were appropriate at one point but have outlived their usefulness. We are not suggesting that you attempt profound modification of your belief system. Rather, we are suggesting that you examine your beliefs and attitudes in those specific situations in which you are having difficulty asserting yourself. Are some of those beliefs erroneous or based on misconceptions? If so, should they be changed?

Since no two individuals subscribe to exactly the same beliefs, there is probably an extremely large and varied set of erroneous or counterproductive beliefs and attitudes which are relevant to assertion training. These counterproductive attitudes and erroneous beliefs can be organized into three categories: beliefs about rights and responsibilities; beliefs about how one should behave or appear to others; and beliefs about probable consequences of behavior. Listed below are several examples from each category. A detailed presentation of counterproductive attitudes and erroneous beliefs and how to cope with them can be found in Discussion Modules 5-18.

Some Examples of Erroneous and/or Counterproductive Beliefs about Rights and Responsibilities Include:

I do not have the right to say no to my friend's requests.
I have the responsibility to provide other people with a clear, logical, and consistent justification for my behavior at all times and in all situations.
I do not have the right to ask others to do things that might inconvenience them.
I do not have the right to disagree with others, especially elders.
I do not have the right to question authority.
I do not have the right to be angry with others, especially not with friends.

The Following are Examples of Counterproductive Beliefs about How One Should Behave or Appear to Others:

I should be loved, liked, or at least admired by practically everyone.
I should be perfect, or at least pretty close, and should not make mistakes.
If I can't say anything nice to a person, I shouldn't say anything at all.

Counterproductive Beliefs about Probable Consequences Often Assume the Form:

If I do or say such and such, then a dire and irreparable consequence will occur. The fact is that the consequences of most social interactions are neutral at worst. Of course, negative reactions to assertive behavior occur on occasion. However, the thought that these reactions are inevitable or even common is unrealistic and counterproductive. There are ways to deal with negative reactions if they occur. This topic is discussed in Chapters Three and Four.

Another counterproductive belief is that *people should provide the consequences I want them to provide . . . or else.* It is this latter belief that often results in increasingly aggressive behavior in a situation.

The problem with counterproductive beliefs is that they serve as rationalizations or excuses that block action or result in inappropriate action. When people subscribe to erroneous beliefs, they seldom question them; but if these beliefs are to be altered, they must be reexamined.

One way to identify and change counterproductive attitudes or beliefs is by reversing your role or perspective in a situation. For example, if you are having difficulty learning to ask a friend for a favor, reverse the perspective. Ask yourself how you would feel if your friend made this request of you. If you believe that it would be reasonable for your friend to make this request—although previously you questioned whether you had this same right—then you have identified a counterproductive belief. Often the realization that you are denying yourself certain privileges and rights that you freely grant to others is sufficient to facilitate assertive behavior in that situation.

At times, reversing your perspective is not sufficient to change a counterproductive belief. In such cases, direct questioning or challenging of the belief is necessary. This questioning can be based on either factual or pragmatic grounds. A factual attack would involve asking: Is the belief true? Why is the belief true? What is the evidence for the belief? For example, if you believe that you do not have the right to be angry with others, you can attack this belief on factual or rational grounds by asking the questions mentioned above. Is it true? Why is this so? What is the evidence for it? Certainly, there is no factual or rational reason for such a belief, and, practically speaking, it is impossible not to be angry with others from time to time.

The belief can be challenged further by a series of questions that dispute its pragmatic value. Does the belief help you to feel the way you want to feel? As we have just said, it is impossible not to feel anger from time to time. Subscribing to the belief that you never feel angry will result only in frustration, since you are trying to achieve something that probably is impossible. Does the belief help you to achieve your goals without hurting others? It probably does not. Usually it is more productive to express justified anger in an assertive manner, there and then, rather than let the angry feelings erode the relationship or explode inappropriately later. Does the belief help you to avoid significant unpleasantness without simultaneously denying your rights? You may avoid some immediate unpleasantness with the other person. However, you have to live with the anger you feel, and you are denying your right to express it.

It is important to realize that some counterproductive attitudes and beliefs are more difficult to change than others and that altering them does take time. Remember, the beliefs were developed over a number of years, and it usually takes time and effort to modify them. What is important is to continuously dispute these attitudes and beliefs each time that you find you are basing your actions on them. Then replace these counterproductive attitudes with more productive attitudes.

How do we recognize a more productive attitude? We would certainly expect that it meets the criteria that we have described in the previous paragraphs. Often a more productive attitude is achieved by adding or subtracting the words "no" or "not" from the counterproductive attitude. For example, "I do *not* have the right to be angry with others" becomes "I do have the right to be angry with others." The important point is to avoid having your behavior ruled by "shoulds," "musts," "oughts," and other absolutes, and instead to base your behavior on your preferences which you implement in an assertive manner (I want _____, I need _____, I prefer _____).

Often, counterproductive beliefs about expected consequences of an assertive act in the real environment can be effectively disarmed by rehearsing the situation first. Rehearsing the assertion may reveal that the recipient of assertive behavior does not respond in the unfavorable manner which you had expected. In addition to rehearsing your behavior, you can also ask the other person how he/she felt or would feel about your behavior. In most instances, you will find that the actual consequences that you receive are not as unfavorable as you had anticipated and that the other person did not feel as disturbed or as inconvenienced as you had feared.

Thought stopping is yet another procedure that can help you cope with counterproductive attitudes or erroneous beliefs. It is especially helpful when you find that you constantly are thinking about a particular belief and can't get it off your mind. By dwelling on the belief, you are inhibited in your efforts to take effective action. In such instances, it may be more helpful to interrupt these beliefs with thought stopping than to spend time attempting to dispute them. Thought stopping* is based on the observation that you cannot have two incompatible or opposing thoughts at the same time. The procedure can help you to control your thoughts and delay thinking about counterproductive beliefs until you are ready to devote your efforts to disputing them.

The procedure is relatively simply and can be learned quickly by following the steps listed below:

Step 1. Close your eyes and begin to think the counterproductive belief.

Step 2. When the counterproductive belief is clearly in mind, yell "stop" out loud, or clap your hands loudly. Since you cannot attend fully to more than one thought at a time, you should find that yelling stop and/or clapping your hands loudly diverts your attention away from the counterproductive thought.

Step 3. It often is helpful to go beyond the simple interruption of your thoughts and to attempt to control the direction of your thinking. In order to gain more control over your thoughts, first repeat Steps 1 and 2. As soon as you have interrupted the counterproductive belief by saying "stop," direct your attention to a thought that is very pleasant to you—for example, relaxing at the beach—or to a productive belief. Try to concentrate on that thought for a few moments.

Step 4. Repeat Steps 1, 2, and 3. This time, however, interrupt your thoughts by saying "stop" to yourself, rather than out loud.

Step 5. Practice Steps 1, 2, and 3, interrupting your counterproductive thoughts at different points. Practice interrupting them as soon as you begin thinking the belief and also after you have been thinking about it for a few moments. By learning to interrupt your counterproductive beliefs at any point in their development, you will be able to stop the counterproductive beliefs in your daily life as soon as you become aware of them.

Step 6. In your daily life, use thought stopping (Steps 2 and 3) each time you find yourself thinking about a counterproductive belief which will not disappear or which you do not have time to dispute. At first, you may find that you have to use thought stopping very frequently (50 times or more). However, if you continue

---

*J. Wolpe, *The Practice of Behavior Therapy*, New York: Pergamon Press, 1973.

to use the procedure conscientiously, we believe that you will be able to develop more control over and reduce the occurrence of counterproductive thoughts in the majority of instances.

In summary, changing a counterproductive belief involves identifying it, disputing or interrupting it, and then adopting a new and more productive belief. Some of the ways that counterproductive beliefs can be challenged or interrupted are:

- Reverse your perspective and explore how you would feel if you were in the other person's position.
- Dispute the belief on factual or rational grounds by asking questions such as, Is the belief true? Why is it true? and/or What evidence is there for this belief?
- Dispute the belief on pragmatic grounds by asking questions such as, Does the belief help you to feel the way you want to feel? Does the belief help you to achieve your goals without hurting others? and Does the belief help you to avoid significant unpleasantness without simultaneously denying your own rights?
- Disarm a counterproductive belief about expected consequences of behavior by role playing the situation and asking the other person to provide feedback on the likely consequences.
- Interrupt stubborn and frequently occurring counterproductive beliefs through thought stopping.

In Discussion Modules 5-18 we discuss in detail some of the common counterproductive beliefs that inhibit people from behaving assertively in particular situations. We also present arguments that dispute each of these beliefs. If you experience difficulty with the situations in Exercise Modules 5-18 due to counterproductive beliefs, reread the corresponding discussion modules as you explore your own beliefs in the situation. Use the procedures outlined in this discussion module as well as any procedures that you discover for yourself as a method for disputing counterproductive beliefs.

Evaluate Your Behavior

After responding to a practice situation in Exercise Modules 5-18, you need to evaluate your behavior if you expect to improve it. Evaluation is important regardless of the method that you have chosen to respond to the practice situations—in writing, role playing, or another. When you begin to transfer your new behavior from the practice situations to real life interactions, evaluation once again will prove to be beneficial. Criteria are discussed below that will help you evaluate the verbal and nonverbal components of assertive behavior. Our clinical experience and research has indicated that these criteria have aided our trainees in learning to behave assertively. Certain cultural or situational variations, however, may necessitate the modification of one or more of these criteria. If you believe it is necessary to modify a criterion for your circumstances, you should observe individuals in your environment who are considered to be assertive. Modify the criterion in relationship to their behavior.

The criteria, as presented in Table 2, cover four areas: the anxiety experienced in the situation; the verbal content of the message; how the message was delivered; and your personal satisfaction with your performance. Your goal is to focus on those criteria which relate to the aspects of behavior you want to change. Begin your evaluation by focusing on only one or two criteria. As you become more proficient in a situation, focus on additional criteria if they seem applicable.

TABLE 2

Criteria for Evaluating Your Behavior

1. Determine your anxiety in the situation
    Suds score
    Eye contact
    Relaxed posture
    Nervous laughter or joking
    Excessive or unrelated head, hand, and body movements
2. Evaluate your verbal content
    Say what you really want to say?
    Comments concise and to the point?
    Comments definitive, specific, and firm?
    No long-winded explanations, excuses, or apologetic behavior
    "I" statements and "feeling talk"
3. Evaluate how you delivered your message
    Almost immediately after the other person spoke
    No hesitancy or stammering
    Appropriate loudness, tone, and inflection
    No whining, pleading, or sarcasm
4. Decide whether you were pleased with your performance

1. Determine your anxiety in the situation

There are five criteria to consider in determining the degree of discomfort you experience while asserting yourself: the Subjective Unit of Disturbance Scale (Suds score),* eye contact, posture, nervous laughter or joking, and excessive or unrelated head, hand, and body movements.

Suds score

The Suds score is used to communicate your subjectively experienced level of anxiety. After responding to each situation, rate yourself using the Suds score. In using the scale, you will rate your level of anxiety from 0, completely relaxed, to 100, very nervous and uptight. In the next three paragraphs, you will learn how to use the Suds score to rate your anxiety.

Imagine when you are completely relaxed and calm. For some people, this occurs while resting or reading a good book. For others, it occurs while lying on the beach or floating in the water. Give your feelings in the situation in which you are most relaxed a rating of "0" Suds.

Next, imagine the situation in which your anxiety is highest. Imagine the feeling of being extremely nervous and uptight. Perhaps in this situation your hands are clammy and cold. You may feel shaky and dizzy, or you may feel quite constricted. For some people, feeling most nervous occurs when someone close has been in an accident; when extreme pressure to achieve is exerted on them (exams, yearly reports, and so on); or when they speak in front of a group. Give the feeling you experience in this situation a rating of "100" Suds.

You have now identified the two end points of the Suds scale: 0 and 100 Suds. Imagine the entire scale (like a ruler) going from 0 Suds, completely relaxed, to 100 Suds, very nervous.

```
0    5    10    15    20    25    30    35 . . . . . 100
completely                                              very
relaxed                                              nervous
```

You now have the entire range of the scale to rate your level of anxiety. To practice using this scale, write your Suds score, at this moment, on the line below

_____

The Suds score will be used throughout the assertion training program. After responding to each situation in which you have practiced assertive behavior, indicate your Suds score. It is important to rate your anxiety level after each rehearsal since one goal of repeated practice is to lower your anxiety (Suds score) as much as possible.

The experience of high levels of anxiety is unpleasant for most people. In addition, the anxiety can inhibit you from saying what you want and can interfere with the way you deliver your message.

The amount which you are able to reduce your Suds score for any situation will depend on a number of factors, including the level of anxiety you generally experience, where your Suds score was on the first practice, what type of assertive behavior is required, and the person to whom you are directing the comment.

If you average 60 Suds during your daily activities, you may find it difficult to reduce your Suds score below this level in most situations. If you believe that you generally experience too much anxiety, you may want to engage in relaxation training before practicing assertive behavior. Relaxation can be achieved through a number of methods, including Jacobson's deep muscle relaxation procedure, yoga, and transcendental meditation. We recommend the deep muscle relaxation procedure. This procedure is outlined in Exercise Module 4.

The amount of anxiety you experience during the first rehearsal of a situation will influence

---

*J. Wolpe, *The Practice of Behavior Therapy.*

the number of rehearsals you need and the difficulty you may experience in reducing your Suds score in that situation. If you have experienced 70 Suds on the first rehearsal, practice the situation until your Suds score decreases noticeably. The number of rehearsals needed usually varies from three to ten.

The type of assertive behavior required in the situation and the person to whom you are directing your comments affect both your initial Suds level and the amount of reduction you can expect. For instance, expressing justified annoyance to one's boss generally creates more anxiety than complimenting one's friend. In addition, most people find that after a number of rehearsals, they can compliment a friend with little or no anxiety, but that expressing justified annoyance to their boss still produces some anxiety. The important point here is that the expression of certain feelings, especially negative feelings, creates anxiety in most people. Thus we do not feel that your goal should be to reach 0 or 5 Suds in all situations. Rather, your goal is to reduce your Suds level to a point where you feel comfortable enough to express yourself.

Eye contact

The impact of your message is affected by the amount of eye contact you maintain with the person to whom you are speaking. When people are anxious, they often tend to look up, down, around, or away from the other person. When you have little or no eye contact with the other person, you appear to be unsure of yourself, and the other person tends not to take your comments seriously. On the other hand, when you look at the person to whom you are speaking, you are generally perceived as more favorable and confident. People tend to look at the person with whom they are conversing more when they are in the listening role than when they are in the speaking role. When you are speaking, it is normal to look away now and then to gather your thoughts and ideas. Research has shown that individuals look at the other person in a conversation about 70 percent of the time.

However, maintaining fairly constant eye contact is quite different than staring at a person. Try not to engage in penetrating stares or hostile glares. Look at the other person to show that you are not only interested in what you are saying but in his/her comments as well. Finally, there are cultures in which maintaining fairly constant eye contact is not effective behavior but instead implies disrespect. The latter is an exception, but if you are a member of one of these cultures you need to adjust this criterion when interacting with members of that culture.

Relaxed posture

Try to maintain a relaxed body stance while asserting yourself. A very rigid and tense appearance or a slouched, almost asleep, position detracts from your message. The rigid or tense body posture often inhibits you from freely expressing yourself, whereas the slouched posture often communicates disinterest to others. Practice finding both comfortable sitting and standing postures that facilitate delivering your message assertively.

Nervous laughter or joking

Nervous laughter or joking does not refer to laughing at appropriate times or telling humorous stories. It refers to those situations in which individuals find themselves laughing or making jokes because they are nervous, embarrassed, or don't know what else to say. Nervous laughter or joking may help you get through some of those situations in which you feel uncomfortable or don't know what to say, but the laughter or joking doesn't help you to express your feelings, ideas, or opinions and can detract from your message. When you begin to joke or laugh nervously, concentrate on saying what you feel rather than the experience of discomfort. One way to accomplish this is by stating that you feel uncomfortable in the situation and that you would appreciate it if the other person would be patient with you.

Excessive or unrelated head, hand, and body movements

Anxiety may be communicated by some individuals through excessive or unrelated head, hand, and body movements. For other individuals, these movements may be due simply to habit, not to feelings of anxiety.

Excessive movements often divert attention away from the verbal message. This does not mean that you shouldn't use your hands, head, or body for emphasis while expressing yourself. Rather, it means that it is important to check whether your nonverbal behavior is adding to or detracting from your comments. This can be accomplished by asking a friend or looking in the mirror.

Unrelated movements tend to confuse the other person(s) in the conversation because they contradict the verbal message. If you find yourself frowning when expressing positive feelings or smiling when expressing annoyance, then you need to develop more consistency between your verbal and nonverbal behavior. Practice making a simple statement, such as "I like you," and then smiling; or practice saying, "I am annoyed with you," and then frowning.

2. Evaluate your verbal content

Say what you really want to say

Your first consideration in evaluating your verbal behavior is to ask yourself whether you said what you really wanted to say. Often people do not say exactly what they want to say, and as a result they feel frustrated and unable to reach their objectives. For instance, telling your neighbor that you are annoyed at him/her for cutting some of the flowers in your garden by saying, "I'm annoyed that you cut my flowers. I don't want that to happen again," is preferable to saying, "My garden really looks barren with all those flowers missing." In the latter comment, you didn't say what you wanted to say.

Make comments concise and to the point

If your comments are concise, to the point, and appropriate to the situation, your message is more likely to be listened to and understood. There is no reason to beat around the bush when you have something to say. State it directly.

When you make a request of a friend, there is no need to engage in a lengthy discourse such as this one: "Sue/Sam, you know the children get out of school early today. What are your children doing this afternoon? Well, maybe mine could do that, too. Would you mind . . . well, I have an appointment and I don't want the kids with me if possible . . . could my children play with yours and . . . well, could you keep an eye on them?"

Instead, be concise and get to the point: "Sue/Sam, I have an appointment at 1:00. Would you watch my children for me until I get home?" When your statements are concise, there is less room for misinterpretation.

Make comments definitive, specific, and firm

If your comments are definitive, specific and firm, they also are more likely to be understood. Be precise in your speech. Give an example, if necessary, to clarify the meaning of your comments. For instance, if you are happy about something and want to express it, instead of just saying, "I'm happy," you could say, "I'm happy about my new promotion." Similarly, if you are annoyed at someone, rather than just saying, "I'm annoyed at you," you might say, "I'm annoyed at you because you continue to overlook my feelings. I told you I didn't want to go over to Bob and Sue's tonight."

No long-winded explanations, excuses, or apologetic behavior

When you express your feelings, you do not have to explain, justify, or make excuses for your behavior. You have the right to feel the way you do and to express it in an appropriate fashion. At times it may be necessary or desirable to include some factual reasons, but it is generally not necessary to engage in long-winded explanations, excuses, or apologetic behavior. For instance, if you are annoyed at your spouse for coming home late, you may say, "I am really annoyed at you for coming home so late. I don't like spending the whole evening alone. I would have at least appreciated a call so I could have made some other plans." However, you need not justify your behavior and make excuses for how you feel by saying, "I know I'm the nervous type and I shouldn't worry so much, but I'm really annoyed you came home so late. I know I've been jumpy ever since my car broke down in the middle of the highway last year, but at least you could have called. I'm sorry I'm so worried about you." When you qualify or make excuses for your behavior, you weaken the impact of your message.

"I" Statements and "Feeling Talk"*

Speaking in the first person and using words that describe your "felt emotions" constitute two additional criteria that you might consider. If you begin your expression with "I," you take responsibility for your feelings and thoughts. You own your feelings and ideas rather than externalize them. Using the "I" statement is particularly helpful when you want to express disappointment, annoyance, or anger. For instance, it may be more appropriate to say, "I am angry because you refused to help me," than to say, "You never help. You are worthless." In the latter statement, you attack the other person. In the former, you express how you feel about his/her behavior.

In "feeling talk," you express how you feel rather than make factual statements. Instead of saying, "Christmas is just a week off" (fact), you could say, "I'll miss you all next week when we're off for Christmas" (feeling talk). Stating how you "feel" about an event or person enhances clear communication with others.

3. Evaluate how you delivered your message

(For use in evaluating role playing or real-life interactions, not for written exercises.) The manner in which you deliver your message also influences how it is received. In certain instances, the way that the verbal message is delivered can be more important than its exact content. The criteria discussed below will help you improve the manner in which you deliver your message.

Almost immediately after the other person spoke

The timing of your delivery influences the way that it is received by the other person. An assertive delivery involves responding almost immediately after the other person has finished

---

*These techniques were developed by A. Salter, *Conditioned Reflex Therapy*. New York: Capricorn Books, 1949.

speaking. Such a delivery communicates that you are sure of yourself and of your point of view. It is important to avoid two extremes of behavior in your delivery: hesitating too long (more than a few seconds) before responding; and interrupting the other person before he/she has finished speaking. The former behavior can be perceived as a lack of confidence in your position by the listener, and the latter behavior can be perceived as disrespectful or aggressive. Hesitating too long before delivering your response can be corrected through repeated practice of assertive interactions. Interruptions, on the other hand, can be reduced or eliminated by counting to two slowly before you respond. In this way, you reduce the likelihood of interrupting the other person before he/she has finished speaking.

Of course, there are several situations in which you must interrupt the other person in order to behave assertively. Terminating a conversation with a person who is monopolizing the situation or interrupting a person who is unjustly criticizing or berating you represent two such examples. In general, however, it is best not to interrupt the other person while he/she is speaking.

No hesitancy or stammering

Often, when you are anxious or do not know what to say, you become hesitant or stumble over your words. Repeated practice will help you become more fluent in your delivery. Obviously, the more fluent and the less hesitant you are the more effective you sound. This criterion is not intended to apply to individuals who have speech problems, such as stuttering.

Appropriate loudness, tone, and inflection

The loudness of your voice should be related to the particular situation in which you find yourself. If you are expressing feelings of love and affection, your voice will be softer than if you are expressing annoyance or anger. In the former situation, very loud speech would be viewed as inappropriate. In all situations, however, it is important that you speak loud enough to be heard. If you speak so softly that others continually have to ask you to repeat what you say, they either will not listen to your message or will not take it seriously. If you speak too softly, practice developing more volume. Ask a friend to listen to you at varying distances and to tell you whether he/she can hear you without difficulty.

The tone and inflection of your voice should be consistent with your verbal content. If you are annoyed, your tone should not be that of a happy-go-lucky person. If you are happy or excited, your speech should not be flat and monotonic. You need to emphasize the important words in your message through inflections.

No whining, pleading, or sarcasm

Whining, pleading, and sarcasm are complex behaviors that are composed of both the content of the message and the manner in which it is delivered. Rather than be direct and honest in their comments, people often manipulate others by whining or pleading with them. Begging someone for what you want is not considered assertive. Whining and pleading often makes the recipient of your message feel guilty. Delivering your message in a sarcastic manner, on the other hand, communicates hostility to the listener. You put the other person down as you sarcastically express your feelings.

4. Decide whether you were pleased with your overall performance

In many ways, this is the most important criterion of all. If you were not pleased with your performance, you are not likely to engage in that behavior in your everyday activities. The main goal of assertion training is not to become proficient in the exercises in this manual but to be able to transfer your new behaviors to your daily interactions. If you are able to complete the exercises in this manual but feel dissatisfied with your responses, you will not be likely to exhibit the responses you have worked on when they are needed later. If you are not pleased with your performance, analyze your behavior and practice the situation again. Consider what it was about your responses you did not like. Consider your rights and responsibilities, the short-term and long-term consequences of the situation, and your attitudes and thoughts. If, after repeated trials, you are still not pleased, go on to other situations. Come back to this situation later and try it again.

Remember that learning new behaviors is not always easy. Therefore it is important that you reward yourself for your efforts. When you have successfully completed an interaction, whether in practice or real life, tell yourself what you have done well. Praise yourself for maintaining good eye contact, for staying calm, or for being concise. Praise yourself for speaking up in an appropriate fashion. Praise yourself for asking your boss for a raise whether you get the raise or not. It is important to reward yourself for engaging in these new behaviors. Rewarding (or reinforcing) yourself for your new behavior will increase the likelihood that you will engage in that behavior again. The manner in which you reinforce or reward yourself may vary. Praising yourself is only one way. Other ways include engaging in an activity that you enjoy following your assertive responses. For instance, you may decide that you need to return faulty merchandise to the store. You have had difficulty in the past with this. You practice the situation a number of times until you are quite pleased with your verbal and nonverbal behaviors. You praise yourself. You then return the merchandise in an assertive fashion. You reward yourself by going to lunch at your favorite downtown cafe.

Actually, in many real life interactions in which you begin to assert yourself, you will find that just being able to speak up and express yourself makes you feel good. You feel rewarded by being able to express your own thoughts and feelings.

Implementing New Behavior in Everyday Interactions

1. Homework assignments and pre-rehearsed interactions

Behaving assertively in practice situations in which the other person is supportive is less difficult than behaving assertively in real-life interactions. The incorporation of homework assignments as well as preplanned and rehearsed interactions into your training will help you transfer assertive behavior into your daily life.

Homework assignments involve a decision to implement a new behavior in real life that you have been practicing in your role playing situations. In a homework assignment, you decide what you will do (for example, ask to borrow a book), with whom (for example, from a close friend), and perhaps when (Tuesday after class). Knowing what you will do and when will make it easier for you to try assertive behavior in your environment. When people learn new habits, it is important that they develop skills and confidence very early in order to help them over difficult times when progress comes more slowly. By determining what you will practice and when, you are attempting to insure that the behavior you practiced in the standard situations will transfer smoothly and easily into real life.

It is important that you select homework assignments that are related to behaviors which you have practiced and with which you feel comfortable. If you have not practiced how to ask favors assertively and/or you do not feel comfortable with this behavior, then don't select it as a homework assignment. Start with easy assignments first and try more difficult assignments later. Remember it is unlikely that you will feel completely satisfied with your performance in each assignment. As we have said before, learning to behave assertively in a situation is similar to learning other skills. When you learned to ride a bike, you probably recall that you had some good days in which you were able to keep your balance most of the time and some bad days in which you fell down a lot. Because you felt that bike riding was an important as well as an enjoyable skill, you continued to practice even though you had your ups and downs. The same is true for learning to behave assertively.

In selecting homework assignments, try to select assignments that are compatible with your everyday needs and with good common sense. For example, if you are practicing asking favors, don't ask for something that you and the other person realize you don't need or for something that is really easier for you to get yourself. Also, don't ask the same person for favors over and over. We would like to help you become more assertive, but we don't want to help you become a nuisance to other people.

In the case of homework assignments, you have preplanned what you want to do, with whom, and when, in an attempt to transfer your new behavior to your everyday life in a smooth manner. This transition also can be facilitated by rehearsing the exact behavior that the homework assignment requires prior to engaging in the assignment. In rehearsing the assignment, we suggest that you practice situations in which the assignment works out positively, negatively, or in a neutral fashion for you. You can do this quite easily by altering the content of the lines of the person with whom you are practicing. In the asking a favor example, you could practice some situations in which the other person grants your request readily, some in which he/she fails to grant your request, and some in which he/she does not give a definite answer. The purpose of varying the consequences is to help you become accustomed to the fact that assertive behavior in the real world does not always result in favorable consequences. Assertive behavior merely increases the likelihood of favorable consequences. We feel that it is important to be aware of this point and to be able to cope with your feelings when an everyday encounter does not work out to your satisfaction. If you can cope with your feelings in such situations, it is less likely that you will become demanding or aggressive.

2. Naturally occurring interactions

As you proceed through this manual, you will become more aware of and more sensitive to situations in your environment in which assertive behavior may be appropriate either for you or for some other person. There are many cues that will indicate these situations to you. For example, you may find that your rights or those of someone else are being violated in an encounter. Perhaps you recognize that someone is making an unreasonable request of you. In another situation, you catch yourself saying something that you do not really believe. In still another situation, you find that your body is becoming tense or that your palms are perspiring, and you realize that you want to express a dissenting point of view. Finally, you find yourself thinking, I should have said such and such in that situation, and you resolve to do so next time it occurs.

In such situations, an assertive response may be appropriate. At such times, we suggest that you appraise the situation (see p. 31). Next, combine the information from this appraisal with an evaluation of your skills and confidence developed by previous practice in similar situations. Then make a decision about whether to be assertive. Our goal is for you to gain the ability to assert yourself when you feel you want to engage in assertive behavior. Obviously the payoff of any assertion training program is the ability to cope effectively with naturally occurring situations that call for assertive behavior. However, these situations should not be tackled prematurely. Begin with the easiest naturally occurring situation and save the hardest ones until you have developed sufficient skills and confidence. The idea is not to avoid or unduly postpone being assertive in naturally occurring situations, but to refrain from jumping in over your head before you are ready.

If you do not perform well either in naturally occurring interactions or homework assignments, you may want to practice these situations further before attempting them again. Another alternative to repeated practice is to observe how people in your environment who are effective in their interpersonal interactions behave in similar situations. Once you know how they behave, you can try to behave in similar ways. This procedure is known as *modeling*, since you attempt to model your behavior after that of people in your environment. In many of the practice situations in Exercise Modules 5-18, we have provided you with examples of model assertive responses as a way of helping you develop new behaviors which you can use in both the practice situations and in your daily life.

3. Record and evaluate homework assignments, pre-rehearsed and naturally occurring interactions

It is helpful if you use the assertion training criteria to evaluate your performance in your everyday interactions. Then record the results in Tables 3 and 4. In the case of naturally occurring interactions, observe and record your performance for about a week prior to beginning the assertion training program. The record for this period of time will provide a baseline or pretraining level against which you can compare your performance after you have begun your assertion training program. You should record your behavior daily. Tables 3 and 4 contain examples of how to complete your daily log. If you place Tables 3 and 4 in a conspicuous location, such as on your refrigerator door, it is likely you will encounter very few instances in which you forget to keep your daily log.

In summary, we have discussed a number of phases and steps that you follow throughout your assertion training program. A summary sheet on these phases appears in Discussion Module 4. You may want to turn to this summary sheet for a moment and review the material you have just read.

TABLE 3A
Daily Log* of Assertive Behavior in Naturally Occurring Interactions

PRIOR TO TRAINING PROGRAM

Date	Behavior	Person	Satisfactory Aspects of Performance	Aspects of Performance that Need Improvement	Overall Evaluation Excellent/Good/Fair/Poor
Sample Entry 3/19/77	Refuse Request	Mary (spouse)	Eye Contact	Content, sarcasm Suds score	Poor

*Make additional copies of this table as needed.

Discussion Module 3

TABLE 3B
Daily Log* of Assertive Behavior in Naturally Occurring Interactions

DURING TRAINING PROGRAM

Date	Behavior	Person	Satisfactory Aspects of Performance	Aspects of Performance that Need Improvement	Overall Evaluation Excellent/Good/Fair/Poor

*Make additional copies of this table as needed.

Discussion Module 3

TABLE 3C
Daily Log* of Assertive Behavior in Naturally Occurring Interactions

AFTER TRAINING PROGRAM

Date	Behavior	Person	Satisfactory Aspects of Performance	Aspects of Performance that Need Improvement	Overall Evaluation Excellent/Good/Fair/Poor

*Make additional copies of this table as needed.

TABLE 4
Daily Log* of Assertive Behavior in Homework Assignments and Prerehearsed Interactions

Date	Behavior	Person	Satisfactory Aspects of Performance	Aspects of Performance that Need Improvements	Overall Evaluation Excellent/Good/Fair/Poor
Sample Entry 4/5/77	Give compliment	Jim (friend)	Verbal content; How I said it—immediately, etc.	Eye contact	Good

*Make additional copies of this table as needed.

EXERCISE MODULE 3
USING THE CRITERIA TO
RATE ANXIETY AND VERBAL CONTENT

In this module, you will practice using the criteria presented in Discussion Module 3 to rate your anxiety level and verbal content.

Rating Your Anxiety

In Discussion Module 3, the Suds score (Subjective Unit of Disturbance Scale) was explained. As you will recall, "0" referred to being completely relaxed and "100" to being very nervous and uptight. Use this scale in intervals of 5 to rate the amount of subjectively experienced anxiety you feel. For example, if a situation makes you feel quite nervous, your Suds score might be 70 or higher. If a situation makes you feel only somewhat nervous, your Suds score might be around 35. Remember, your Suds score is based on your feelings, and only you know how relaxed or anxious you feel in a situation.

To practice using the Suds score, a number of situations will be described. For each situation, read the description of that scene and then imagine that this situation is happening to you. After you imagine the situation, write down the amount of anxiety (Suds score) you felt. When imagining yourself in that situation, try to write how you would feel if that situation were actually occurring. Finally, if you were nervous or uptight while imagining that scene, try to pinpoint those parts of your body in which you felt most anxious. Did you feel queasy or jittery in your stomach? Was your throat tight? Were your hands cold or sweaty? Did your head ache? Did your eye twitch? If you can locate the area or areas in which you feel most anxious, then you can use this information when you practice the relaxation exercises in Exercise Module 4.

Three situations are presented below. Try to imagine yourself in each of the situations.

Situation 1

You bought a pair of wash-and-wear slacks at a department store last week. You wore them just once and then washed them according to the directions. You put them on today and discover they have shrunk considerably. Now, imagine that you are returning the slacks to the salesperson. As you ask to exchange the slacks, the salesperson implies that you are responsible for the shrinkage.

What was your Suds score in Situation 1? _____

If you were anxious or uptight in this situation, in what parts of your body did you feel this anxiety (e.g., tightness in throat, etc.)?

_____
_____

Describe how you would feel if this situation actually were occurring.

_____
_____

Situation 2

You handed in a project report to your supervisor/professor two weeks ago. You worked quite hard on both the project and the report. You know that you did a good job on this assignment. Imagine that your supervisor/professor approaches when you are chatting with some co-workers/classmates and compliments you for doing an excellent job. He/she says that your report is one of the most complete ones that he/she has ever seen. He/she also says that the project was well conceived and competently carried out in each and every detail. He/she ends by saying it is a pleasure to have you on his/her staff/class.

What was your Suds score in Situation 2? _____

If you were anxious or uptight in this situation, in what parts of your body did you feel this anxiety (e.g., tightness in your throat)?

_____
_____

Describe how you would feel if this situation actually were occurring.

_____
_____

Situation 3

At 4 P.M., a friend asks if he/she could borrow your car for half an hour since his/her car is in the shop and he/she needs to pick up a package at the post office. You say it is okay as long as he/she is back by 5 P.M., because you have a dinner engagement at 6 P.M. Your friend returns at 6:15 P.M. and apologizes that he/she lost track of the time when he/she bumped into some old friends at the post office. Imagine telling your friend that you are quite annoyed at him/her and that there is no reason that he/she should have been so inconsiderate of your plans.

What was your Suds score in Situation 3? _____

If you were anxious or uptight in this situation, in what parts of your body did you feel this anxiety (e.g., tightness in your throat)?

_____
_____

Describe how you would feel if this situation actually were occurring.

_____
_____

If you were able to imagine yourself in these three situations, you should now have a better idea of how to use the Suds score. If you had difficulty imagining yourself in these situations, try the following exercise. Read the situation over and then respond aloud as if the other person were standing there with you. Then answer the three questions that follow each situation.

Rating Verbal Content

A number of examples are provided to give you practice rating verbal content using the criteria described in Discussion Module 3. Rate each comment delivered by the person referred to as "you" in the situation. Then check your ratings against ours. In each exercise, do not be concerned if the second person's behavior is not assertive.

When rating each comment, first decide whether it is aggressive or not. If it is aggressive, indicate why. Does it include threats, insults, verbal assaults, and so on? If the comment is not aggressive, then use the criteria in Table 2 for evaluating verbal content. These criteria are summarized for you below.

    Did "you" say what "you" really wanted to say?
    Were the comments concise, to the point, and appropriately assertive to the situation?
    Were the comments definitive, specific, and firm?
    Did "you" avoid long-winded explanations, excuses, and apologetic behavior?
    Did "you" use "I" statements and "feeling talk" when appropriate?

Situations for Rating Verbal Content

Remember to rate only the comments designated as "you."

Situation 1—Standing up for your Rights with a Salesperson

You bought a pair of wash-and-wear slacks at a department store last week. You wore them just once and then washed them according to the directions. You put them on today and discover they have shrunk considerably. You have decided to return the slacks. You want to either exchange them or receive a refund. You are approaching the salesperson now.

	Salesperson:	Good afternoon. May I help you?
Comment 1	*You:*	Well . . . maybe . . . er . . . I think so . . . Uh. Do you have any slacks in size 32?
	Salesperson:	Yes, right over here.
Comment 2	*You:*	Are they wash-and-wear?
	Salesperson:	Some are.
Comment 3	*You:*	Well, I don't think I want wash-and-wear pants. They aren't as good as they say. Many people have problems with them. They don't hold up like they should. You know what I mean. Have you ever bought any yourself?
	Salesperson:	These are the finest wash-and-wear. Why don't you try a pair? They are on special today.
Comment 4	*You:*	I can see why they are (*raising voice*). You are trying to push those faulty slacks on the consumer. You are pretty clever putting them on sale. Here's another pair to put on sale. You know what you can do with these. (*You throw slacks on counter and leave.*)

Rate the comments

Comment 1: _____

_____

Comment 2: _____

_____

Comment 3: _____

_____

Comment 4: _____

_____

Our rating of the comments

Comment 1: You begin by saying "you think" and "maybe" the salesperson can help you, rather than saying, "Yes, you can." You seem to doubt that he/she can help you. You are not definitive. Then you ask for size 32 slacks. This is not the point you came to make.

Comment 2: Asking, "Are they wash-and-wear," again is not the point you want to make. You are just stalling for time. The salesperson does not know what is in your bag or even know that you have something to return. You are not saying what you want to say.

Comment 3: You give a long-winded explanation on why you don't want wash-and-wear slacks. The point that you should be making is, "I bought a pair of wash-and-wear slacks, and they have shrunk considerably. I want to return them."

Comment 4: Having rambled on for a while and with no satisfaction from the salesperson, you begin to get very angry. However, you have not stated your complaint. You probably are unaware that you have not told the salesperson what you want. As a result, he/she is probably quite confused when you become aggressive. You accuse him/her of pushing off faulty merchandise on the public. You imply he/she is sneaky, and then you tell him/her what he/she can do with them. You have accused the salesperson and have verbally assaulted him/her. Both were inappropriate.

Exercise Module 3

Situation 1—Five New Comments are Presented for You to Evaluate

	Salesperson:	Good afternoon. May I help you?
Comment 5	*You*:	Yes, you can. I'd like to return these slacks because they shrank when I washed them.
	Salesperson:	Are they wash and wear?
Comment 6	*You*:	Yes and I read the directions very carefully. I have bought wash-and-wear clothes before. I have a new washing machine with all those fancy dials so I know I washed them correctly. All my other wash-and-wears were fine. My friend said it must be your slacks. He/she should know because he/she owns a laundromat.
	Salesperson:	These are the finest wash-and-wear slacks made.
Comment 7	*You*:	That may be so, but I'd like to return them.
	Salesperson:	Perhaps you bought the wrong size.
Comment 8	*You*:	I doubt that. I'd like to return them.
	Salesperson:	All right, how much were they? Here is your money. I'm sorry about the inconvenience.
Comment 9	*You*:	Thank you. Good day.

Rate the comments

Comment 5: _____

Comment 6: _____

Comment 7: _____

Comment 8: _____

Comment 9: _____

Our rating of the comments

Comment 5: This comment is concise, to the point, and appropriately assertive to the situation. You definitively state what you want and offer only a factual reason. Your introductory comments are assertive.

Comment 6: Rather than sticking to the point that you want to return the slacks, you get sidetracked. You give a long-winded explanation, perhaps to justify your behavior to the salesperson. You need not give long-winded explanations or make excuses for returning the slacks. The fact that the slacks shrank after being washed according to the directions is the only explanation needed.

Comments 7 and 8: In both of these comments, you remain concise and to the point. You are firm and definitive. You merely repeat, "I'd like to return them." Simply repeating your message verbatim a number of times is a good way of staying on target. Repeating your message is often referred to as the broken record technique. If you have something to say and the other party responds as if he/she did not hear you, then just replay your message. You need not feel that you have to vary the content of what you say. If you believe that it is not acceptable to simply repeat your message, then you tend to make excuses and/or long-winded explanations, as in Comment 6. The problem with excuses is that they are easily disputed by others, and you often find yourself with little left to say.

Comment 9: This comment is appropriately assertive to the situation. You thank the salesperson for returning your money and proceed on your way.

Supplemental Exercise for Situation 1

Reread the two sets of responses for Situation 1. Then answer the following questions. Discuss your answers with someone else if possible.

Contrast how you would feel after the first comment in each of the two situations.

_____
_____

Contrast how you would feel at the conclusion of each version of Situation 1.

_____
_____

In the future, what would be your relationship with this store after each interaction?

_____
_____

Situation 2–Receiving a Compliment from a Supervisor/Professor

You handed in a project report to your supervisor/professor two weeks ago. You worked quite hard on both the project and the report. You know that you did a good job on this assignment. Your supervisor/professor approaches you when you are chatting with some co-workers/classmates in the hall.

	Supervisor/Prof:	You did an excellent job on that report you gave me last week. It is one of the best projects I've ever seen.
Comment 1	*You*:	Oh, uh . . . it wasn't much.
	Supervisor/Prof:	The project was well conceived and competently carried out in each and every detail.
Comment 2	*You*:	It wasn't really a very difficult task.
	Supervisor/Prof:	It's a pleasure to have you on my staff/in my class.
Comment 3	*You*:	Well, I'm really glad that I work with you/that I'm in your class.

Rate the comments

Comment 1: _____

Comment 2: _____

Comment 3: _____

Our rating of the comments

Comment 1: You apologize for your efforts saying, "It wasn't much." You need not apologize for doing a good job. An appropriately assertive comment would include at least an acknowledgement of the compliment—"Thank you."

Comment 2: Again, you put yourself down (apologize for your work). You say, "It wasn't a very difficult task," even though you know that you worked quite hard on the assignment. In addition, by not accepting the compliment in Comments 1 and 2, you imply that your supervisor's/professor's judgment is faulty.

Comment 3: Assuming that your comment is sincere, it seems more appropriate to say it after you have accepted your supervisor's/professor's compliment. The objective of this situation is to accept your supervisor's/professor's praise of your work. However, since you either feel embarrassed or don't know what to say, you compliment him/her instead.

Situation 2–Three new comments are presented for you to evaluate

	Supervisor/Prof:	You did an excellent job on that report you gave me last week. It is one of the best projects I've ever seen.
Comment 4	*You:*	I really appreciate that since I worked quite hard on that project.
	Supervisor/Prof:	The project was well conceived and competently carried out in each and every detail.
Comment 5	*You:*	Thank you. I tried not to overlook anything.
	Supervisor/Prof:	It's a pleasure to have you on my staff/in my class.
Comment 6	*You:*	Thanks again. This job/class has worked out quite well for me.

Rate the comments

Comment 4: _____

_____

Comment 5: _____

_____

Comment 6: _____

_____

Our rating of the comments

Comment 4: You accept the compliment by telling your supervisor/professor that you appreciated his/her praise. In addition, you gave a factual reason, "I worked quite hard," for your appreciation of his/her remarks. Your remarks are concise and to the point.

Comment 5: In this instance, you accept his/her praise with a simple thank you. You concur with his/her judgment by stating the fact that you tried not to overlook anything.

Comment 6: Again, you accept the compliment and make a brief statement that is concise and appropriate to the situation.

Situation 3—Expressing Annoyance to a Friend

At 4 P.M., a friend asks if he/she could borrow your car for half an hour since his/her car is in the shop and he/she needs to pick up a package at the post office. You say okay as long as he/she is back by 5 P.M., because you have a dinner engagement at 6 P.M. Your friend does not return until 6:15 P.M. You are quite annoyed.

	Friend:	Here's your keys. Thanks.
Comment 1	*You*:	Do you know what time it is?
	Friend:	No, but I guess I'm a little late.
Comment 2	*You*:	It's 6:15 P.M. Where were you?
	Friend:	I bumped into some old friends at the post office. I guess I lost track of the time.
Comment 3	*You*:	Well . . . er . . . who were they? . . . No . . . I have to go now.
	Friend:	See you later. Have a good time.

Rate the comments

Comment 1: _____

_____

Comment 2: _____

_____

Comment 3: _____

_____

Our rating of the comments

Comment 1: In this comment, you do not say what you really want to say. Your friend is aware that more than half an hour has passed since he/she left. The point to be made is that you are annoyed since it is now 6:15 P.M., and you asked that he/she return by 5 P.M. Asking your friend whether he/she "knows what time it is" is not a firm approach to the situation.

Comment 2: Unless he/she was in an accident or something catastrophic had occurred, his/her whereabouts for the last two hours and fifteen minutes are immaterial. If an accident had occurred, you probably would have been notified, or he/she would have immediately indicated the situation to you upon returning. If you are annoyed, express this directly to your friend. "I am quite annoyed. I asked you to return my car by 5 P.M., so I could go to my dinner engagement."

Comment 3: You realize that who he/she bumped into is not important. However, you leave without saying what you really wanted to say. You did not express your annoyance.

Situation 3–Three new comments are presented for you to evaluate

	Friend:	Here's your keys. Thanks.
Comment 4	*You*:	John/Joan, I'm quite annoyed at you. I told you I needed to be at a dinner by 6 P.M. It is now 6:15.
	Friend:	I guess I'm a little late.
Comment 5	*You*:	Yes. I asked you to return by 5 P.M. I feel that you took advantage of me in this situation.
	Friend:	I bumped into some old friends at the post office. I guess I lost track of the time.
Comment 6	*You*:	I don't think you were considerate of my needs, and I hope this doesn't happen again. I need to go now.
	Friend:	I understand how you must feel. I hope you can still enjoy your dinner. See you later.

Rate the comments

Comment 4: _____

Comment 5: _____

Comment 6: _____

Our rating of the comments

Comment 4: You assert yourself immediately by stating how you feel, "I'm quite annoyed." You say what you really wanted to say. You come right to the point. You give a factual reason, but not a long-winded sermon, to your friend. You use "I talk," thereby owning your feelings.

Comment 5: In an appropriate manner, you tell your friend how you feel, "taken advantage of." You are concise, to the point, firm, and definitive.

Comment 6: You conclude by restating how you feel and by indicating what you expect from your friend in the future ("I hope this doesn't happen again"). You do not become aggressive at any time. No threats, insults, or name calling occur. Further, you state that you must leave now while indicating that you are not planning to terminate the relationship. You have said what you really want to say.

We hope that our comments on the above situations will help you to evaluate more accurately your verbal responses in the practice situations of Exercise Modules 5-18. If you have difficulty rating your behavior, review this module and the material on verbal content in Discussion Module 3.

EXERCISE MODULE 4
TRAINING IN DEEP MUSCLE RELAXATION

We have mentioned that sometimes you may experience difficulty asserting yourself in a situation because you become overly anxious. The anxiety that you experience may inhibit you from being able to say what you want to say. At times you even may choose to completely avoid expressing yourself rather than experience the anxiety. There are a number of ways to learn to deal with this anxiety. Among the ways to decrease your anxiety are: disputing counterproductive attitudes and erroneous beliefs, repeatedly practicing what to say and how to say it (role playing), and learning to relax your body.

This exercise module presents a procedure for learning to systematically relax your muscles. When you are anxious or uptight, you may appear rigid in posture and feel a great deal of muscle tension. Conversely, when you are relaxed and feel at ease in a situation there is a minimum amount of muscle tension.

Training in deep-muscle relaxation* has long been recognized as an effective means of coping with stress and reducing anxiety. It is based on the premise that you cannot be both tense and relaxed at the same time, and that by learning to relax various muscle groups in the body, you can learn to cope more effectively with stress.

Learning deep-muscle relaxation is similar to learning any other skill in that it takes regular practice. After you understand deep muscle relaxation, we suggest that you practice it at least once a day for twenty to thirty minutes. You may find it helpful to follow the steps listed below in developing your own relaxation training procedures.

Step 1. Record the relaxation procedures on audiotape

Many people find it helpful to record the relaxation procedures on audiotape and to use the tape while they are practicing. You may wish to make the tape yourself, or you may ask someone who has a very calm, soothing voice to make the tape for you.

The tape should begin by asking you to close your eyes, get comfortable in your chair, and just relax. Then directions should be given to relax each of the muscles in Table 5 in the order that is shown. You will find the following format helpful. "Tense the muscles _____." (Leave a five- to seven-second pause on the tape so you can hold the tension.) "Now let go and relax completely." (Leave a twenty- to thirty-second pause on the tape for relaxation.)

You may wish to record two relaxation tapes, one in which each muscle group is tensed and relaxed twice before proceeding to the next muscle group, and one in which each group is tensed and relaxed only once. After giving directions for the final muscle group (number 16) on each tape, you may want to give directions to repeat the deep-breathing exercise (number 12) once or twice, since many people find this procedure very relaxing. In addition, you may want to give directions at the end of the tape to imagine yourself in a very pleasant scene, such as lying in the sun at the beach (if this is pleasant to you), since such imagery often is quite relaxing.

To conclude the relaxation tape, you may want to add the following: "Now you have been relaxing very well, and in a moment I shall ask you to open your eyes. When you do so, you will be alert, yet relaxed. I will count backwards from five to one. When I reach one, you will open your eyes: 5...4...3...2...1."

If you do not have a tape recorder or prefer not to use one, you still can follow the procedures we have outlined. Use Table 5 and alternately tense each muscle group for five to seven seconds and then relax it for twenty to thirty seconds.

---

*This procedure was developed by E. Jacobson, *Progressive Relaxation*. Chicago: University of Chicago Press, 1938.

TABLE 5

Order of Major Muscle Groups to be Relaxed

1. Tense the muscles in your right hand by making a fist.
2. Tense the muscles in your right upper arm. Bend your arm at the elbow and make a muscle.
3. Tense the muscles in your left hand by making a fist.
4. Tense the muscles in your left upper arm. Bend your arm at the elbow and make a muscle.
5. Tense the muscles in your forehead by frowning.
6. Tense the muscles in your eyes by closing your eyes tightly.
7. Tense the muscles in your nose by wrinkling it.
8. Tense the muscles in your lips and lower face by pressing your lips together tightly and forcing your tongue against the top of your mouth.
9. Tense the muscles in your jaw by clenching your teeth together.
10. Tense the muscles in your neck by attempting to look directly above you.
11. Tense the muscles in your shoulders and upper back by shrugging your shoulders.
12. Tense the muscles in your chest by taking a deep breath and holding it.
13. Tense the muscles in the small of your back by arching up your back.
14. Tense the muscles in your abdomen by either pushing those muscles out or pulling them in.
15. Tense the muscles in your buttocks and thighs by pressing your heels into the floor.
16. Tense the muscles in your ankles and calves by pointing them away from your body.

Step 2. Prepare yourself to practice deep-muscle relaxation

Select a time and a place in which you can practice relaxation daily without interruption. Find a comfortable, high-back, padded armchair or a bed to practice in. Remove your contact lenses if you wear them; loosen tight clothing. If you are sitting in a chair, plant both feet firmly on the floor. Record your Suds score before beginning the relaxation procedures.

Step 3. Practice using the tape in which each muscle group is repeated twice (5 to 7 days)

While tensing your muscles, do not tense them so tightly that you develop a muscle cramp. Mild tension is all that is needed. The purpose of tension is only to highlight the sensations of relaxation. When relaxing each muscle, you may find it helpful to count slowly: 1 . . . 2 . . . 3, etc. With each count, try to unwind or let go of the tension more and more. It is this unwinding that is important. Note your Suds score at the end of each session. A drop of 15 to 20 Suds after the first practice session is not uncommon. After each session, notice whether any muscles are still tense. If so, were you sitting in an uncomfortable position, or do you need to devote additional attention to relaxing that muscle group? As you continue your practice sessions, you will find that you relax more and more deeply in a shorter time period.

Step 4. Practice using the tape in which each muscle group is repeated only once (5 to 7 days)

As you develop skills in deep muscle relaxation, switch to the tape in which each muscle group is tensed and relaxed once. If you are not using an audiotape, simply practice tensing and relaxing each muscle group in Table 5 only once. Record your Suds score after each practice session.

Step 5. Practice relaxing each muscle group without tensing it (5 to 7 days)

As you progress in your training program, you will find it is no longer necessary for you to tense each muscle group before relaxing it. You can learn to relax without the aid of tensing. If you find that it is too large a step to depart from the use of a tape at the same time that you eliminate tensing from the procedure, it may be helpful to separate these steps. You can make a tape which has relaxation instructions only (no tensing instructions) and use it for several days. Then phase the tape out altogether. Record your Suds score after each practice session.

Step 6. Practice differential relaxation

In your day-to-day interactions, it is not feasible to sit down in a chair and go through the entire deep-muscle relaxation procedure each time you experience anxiety. However, it is possible to relax individual muscle groups that are not being used. For example, if you have to speak in front of a group, it is possible to use deep-breathing exercises prior to the presentation to help control your anxiety. If you are seated, it is also possible to relax your legs or abdomen during the presentation. You should attempt to relax muscles that are not used during stressful situations. Through differential relaxation, you will be able to inhibit some of the feelings of tension or anxiety that you are experiencing. It is helpful to practice differential relaxation at home before using it in your daily interactions. Remember to record your

Suds score each time in order to determine the progress that you are making in coping with anxiety.

Differential relaxation is the most important aspect of deep muscle relaxation training. Also, it is probably the most difficult to master. However, with practice, you will develop skill in using differential deep muscle relaxation, breathing exercises, and the imagination of pleasant scenes to help you to control your Suds level in stressful encounters. Some individuals may find that they are still uncomfortable asserting themselves after both repeated practice and relaxation training. In such instances, it may be helpful to consult a counselor for assistance.

Discussion Module **4**

Personalizing Your Program: Discussion and Exercise Modules 5-18

Discussion and Exercise Modules 5-18 are designed to correspond to one another. For instance, Discussion Module 5 provides information on the rights, responsibilities, and rationale involved in giving and receiving compliments, whereas Exercise Module 5 provides a number of situations for you to practice giving and receiving compliments. We suggest that when you choose a particular exercise module, you first read its corresponding discussion module and the introductory comments for the chapter in which the discussion module is found.

You should note that each of the Discussion and Exercise Modules 5-13 corresponds to one of the behaviors represented in the rows of the Assertion Self-Assessment Table, whereas Modules 14-18 correspond to a number of the persons represented in the columns of the Table. We suggest that you complete at least those discussion and exercise modules which correspond to the behaviors and persons in Table 1 with which you had difficulty asserting yourself. For example, if your self-assessment revealed that you have difficulty in either giving or receiving compliments, read and complete the material in Discussion and Exercise Module 5.

As you proceed through the exercise modules, you will find that situations have not been provided for each of the persons listed in the Self-Assessment Table. For instance, you may have indicated in your self-assessment that you feel extremely anxious while accepting compliments from your parents. However, you do not find such a situation in Exercise Module 5. In this case, you could insert parent in place of one of the role figures who is provided in the situations. Another alternative would be for you to develop your own situation in the blank page provided in the exercise module.

In each exercise module, a number of situations are described. For each situation, a number of responses follow. Respond to the series of statements as if you were engaging in an ongoing conversation with the other person. As you will recall from Discussion Module 3, you can respond to the situations in a variety of ways: writing, role playing, and so on. Regardless of the manner in which you respond to the situations, repeated practice is important in learning to become assertive.

A model of appropriate assertive behavior is included in each exercise module. The purpose of the model is to help you behave assertively in the situations that are presented.

Before you begin your assertion training program, we want to remind you about the importance of behaving appropriately and responsibly—that is, assertively. Assertive behavior involves expressing your rights, feelings, and opinions without simultaneously denying or ignoring the rights, feelings, and opinions of others. Assertive behavior is not aggressive behavior, and it is important to remember this distinction throughout your training program.

A summary sheet that reviews the phases for learning assertive behavior is presented on the following page. The sheet includes the criteria for evaluating your behavior, and it can be detached and used as a guide for practicing the situations presented in Exercise Modules 5-18.

Finally, note that the procedures for changing counterproductive beliefs and the criteria for evaluating your behavior also appear on a separate page at the end of this module. We suggest that you cut them out and paste them on the front and back of a 3 x 5 card. Carry the card in your pocket or purse so that you can use it to rate your behavior in everyday interactions.

SUMMARY SHEET
Phases of Assertion Training

I. *Appraise the Situation*
   1. Determine what you believe the rights and responsibilities are of the various parties in the situation.
   2. Determine the probable short-term and long-term consequences of various courses of action.
   3. Decide how you will behave in the situation.

II. *Experiment with New Behaviors and Attitudes in Practice Situations*
   1. Try out your new behavior in the situations provided. Respond aloud or in writing to the standard lines; role play with another person; etc. Practice each situation as many times as necessary.
   2. Write your own situations to practice.
   3. Dispute erroneous beliefs and counterproductive attitudes and replace them with more accurate and productive beliefs.
      Reverse your perspective. How would you feel in the other person's position?
      Is the belief true? Why is it true? What evidence supports the belief?
      Does the belief help you to feel the way you want to feel?
      Does the belief help you to achieve your goals without hurting others?
      Does the belief help you to avoid significant unpleasantness without simultaneously denying your own rights?
      Ask for opinions from others concerning the likely impact and consequences of your behavior.
      Use thought stopping to interrupt stubborn and frequently occurring counterproductive beliefs.

III. *Evalute Your Behavior*
   1. Determine your anxiety in the situation. (Use relaxation training if necessary)
      Suds score
      Eye contact
      Relaxed posture
      Nervous laughter or joking
      Excessive or unrelated head, hand, and body movements
   2. Evaluate your verbal content.
      Did you say what you really wanted to say?
      Were your comments concise, to the point, appropriately assertive to the situation?
      Were your comments definitive, specific, and firm?
      Did you avoid long-winded explanations, excuses, and apologetic behavior?
      Did you use "I" statements and "feeling talk" when appropriate?
   3. Evaluate how you delivered your message.
      Did you reply almost immediately after the other person spoke?
      Was there hesitancy or stammering in your voice?
      Were your volume, tone, and inflection appropriate?
      Was there any whining, pleading, or sarcasm in your voice?
   4. Decide whether you were pleased with your overall performance in the situation.

IV. *Implement New Behavior in Everyday Interactions*
   1. Decide to assert yourself in a real-life situation. Practice that situation as a homework assignment.
   2. Begin to assert yourself in naturally occurring interactions, being careful not to jump in over your head.

Discussion Module 4

3. Record and evaluate homework assignments, prerehearsed, and naturally occurring interactions using Tables 3 and 4 in Discussion Module 3.

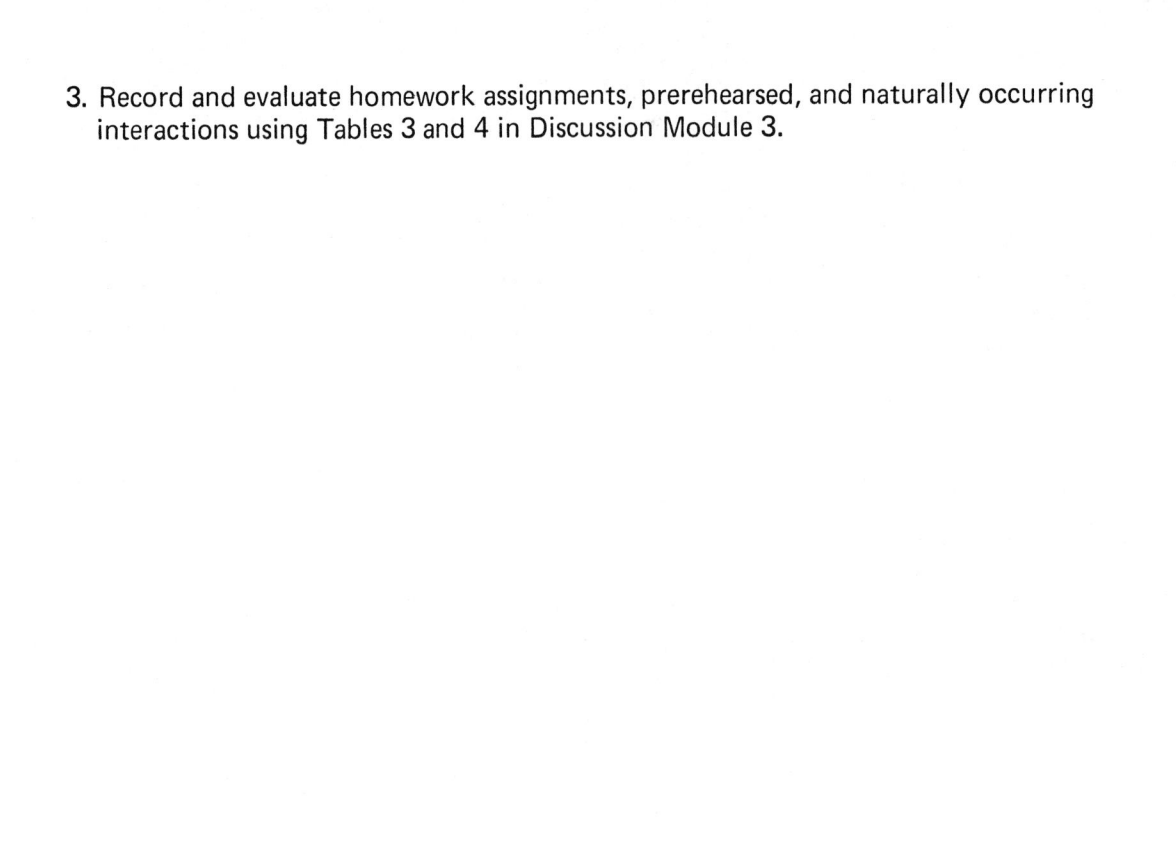

Cut out the criteria for evaluating your behavior and the ways to dispute counterproductive attitudes and beliefs. Paste them on the front and back of a 3 x 5 card which you can carry in your pocket or purse.

How anxious or relaxed were you?
    Suds score? Eye contact? Relaxed posture?
    Nervous laughter or joking?
    Excessive or unrelated head, hand, and body movements?
What did you say?
    Say what you really wanted to say?
    Comments concise, to the point and appropriate?
    Comments definitive, specific, and firm?
    Perhaps a factual reason, but no long-winded explanations, excuses, or apologetic behavior?
    Use "I" statements and "feeling talk" when appropriate?
How did you say it?
    Almost immediately after the other person spoke?
    No hesitancy or stammering in your voice?
    Volume, tone, and inflection appropriate?
    No whining, pleading, or sarcasm?
Were you pleased with your overall performance?

Ways to dispute counterproductive attitudes and beliefs.
    Reverse your perspective. How would you feel in the other person's position?
    Is the belief true? Why is it true? What evidence supports the belief?
    Does the belief help you to feel the way you want to feel?
    Does the belief help you to achieve your goals without hurting others?
    Does the belief help you to avoid significant unpleasantness without simultaneously denying your own rights?
    Ask for opinions from others concerning the likely impact and consequences of your behavior.
    Use thought stopping to interrupt stubborn and frequently occurring beliefs.

Discussion Module 4

Chapter 2

Expressing Positive Feelings

Under positive feelings, we have listed a diverse group of behaviors, which include giving and receiving compliments, making requests, expressing love and affection, and initiating and maintaining conversations. These behaviors share in common an active, positive orientation that involves initiating contact with one's environment.

Discussion Module **5**

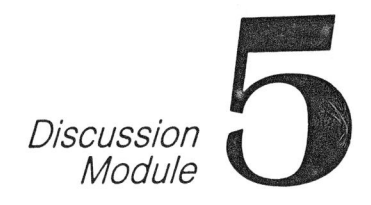

Giving and Receiving Compliments

Giving Compliments

Being able to give compliments and express appreciation in an assertive manner is an important skill. We feel that people have the right to provide positive feedback to others about specific aspects of behavior, dress, and so on, which they appreciate. For example, "Mary, it was very kind of you to run that errand for me when you realized that I was going to be late." If you feel warm and complimentary toward someone or about something, you have the right to express that feeling regardless of whether others share your feelings. It is a rare occasion indeed when a compliment hurts another person.

There undoubtedly are many reasons why it is important to give compliments and to express appreciation when it is justified. Among them are the following:

1. Other people enjoy hearing sincere, positive expressions about how you feel about them.
2. Expressing compliments results in deepening and strengthening the relationship between two people.
3. When people are complimented, it is less likely that they will feel unappreciated or taken for granted.
4. Those instances in which you have to express negative feelings or stand up for legitimate rights with an individual are less likely to result in a high-pitched, emotional confrontation if they occur in a relationship in which you previously have complimented the individual about other aspects of his/her behavior. In other words,

negative feedback is received more favorably and is less likely to be threatening if a generally positive climate exists between the people involved.

Often when people have difficulty giving compliments, it is because they hold certain misconceptions or counterproductive attitudes that interfere with their behavior. As we have mentioned before, these attitudes often are idiosyncratic, but they must be disputed when they are encountered, and they must be replaced with more productive attitudes.

Listed below are some of the common counterproductive attitudes that we have encountered that prevent people from giving compliments when they are merited. Each of the counterproductive attitudes is followed by an internal dialogue that can be used for disputing the attitude and for arriving at a more productive view. In exploring your own beliefs and in reading the beliefs listed below, you may find it helpful to refer to Discussion Module 3 to review the methods for changing misconceptions and counterproductive beliefs.

Counterproductive beliefs about how I should behave or appear to others

I shouldn't have to compliment others. They should know how I feel from the way I act. Besides, I feel funny complimenting them.
What is the evidence for this? What basis do I have for believing that other people are mind readers and that they know how I feel about them? They could interpret (misinterpret) my actions in more than one way. A sincere compliment would let them know how I feel and would be less likely to be subject to misunderstanding. Sure, I feel funny about complimenting others. It's something I rarely do, so of course I'll feel funny for a while. No, I shouldn't be required to give compliments, but, if I want to, I will. It will make the other person feel good to hear the compliment, and it will make me feel good to give it, if that's what I want to do.

Why should I compliment him/her? He/she is getting paid for the work.
Does this belief help me to achieve my goals and to do so without hurting others? I guess it doesn't really hurt the other person that much if I don't compliment him/her. But, I know that people respond well to a sincere expression of satisfaction, and if I feel that he/she merits a compliment, then I ought to be able to give one if I want to.
How do I feel when I'm getting paid for something? I guess almost everyone appreciates a kind word now and then. Money isn't the only reward for me.

Counterproductive beliefs about the probable consequences of behavior

If I go around complimenting people and telling them how much I appreciate them, they will think that I want something from them. Also, they may think that I am insincere.
Why is this true? I'm only talking about giving compliments when I feel they are warranted, not giving them ad nauseam. I suppose that I really give too few compliments. When was the last time that someone acted suspicious about a compliment? Don't people usually enjoy hearing compliments? Maybe I ought to ask someone how they would feel if I gave compliments more frequently.

I don't compliment other people because most people don't know how to take a compliment gracefully; they get all flustered or embarrassed.
This belief doesn't help me to feel the way I want to feel, does it? I want to be able to give compliments and to feel comfortable doing so. Why do I think that I am responsible for the other person's behavior? I can't control the other person's reactions. Besides, if he/she

becomes embarrassed, I can say, "I just wanted you to know that this is the way I feel." I cannot and should not force the other person to accept the compliment or to give me one in return. All I can do is give the compliment, and that's that.

Receiving Compliments

Receiving a compliment is similar to giving a compliment in that the manner in which it is handled influences both individuals in the interchange. It is important to accept a compliment gracefully. A compliment is a subjective evaluation by another person. If you do not accept the compliment or you make it difficult for the other person to give it, you are either questioning the validity of that judgment or the honesty of the person giving the compliment. For example, assume that a person compliments you on a suit that you are wearing. Your response is, "This old thing?" or "You don't really mean that." What your response communicates is either that the person giving the compliment has poor taste in clothing or that he/she is an insincere flatterer. Of course, there are situations in which a compliment is undeserved, and you assert yourself and indicate that you appreciate the compliment but that it is not warranted (for example, Sally/Joe did the report for which you are being complimented).

Accepting a compliment involves at a minimum acknowledging it with a simple thank you, a smile, or a sentence such as, "I appreciate hearing that." In addition, if you agree with the compliment, you may wish to comment briefly on it: "I'm glad you like my suit. It is my favorite." "I'm pleased that you liked the report. I worked very hard on it, and I was pleased with the results."

Once again, people often subscribe to counterproductive attitudes that make it difficult for them to accept compliments. A few of these attitudes, followed by internal dialogues which may be used to dispute them, are listed below.

Counterproductive beliefs about rights and responsibilities

People really shouldn't compliment me because I usually don't deserve it.
Why is this so? Why do I think I'm so undeserving? After all, if that's the other person's opinion, then he/she is entitled to it. Isn't it rather impolite to dispute it? If he/she really feels that way, it probably makes him/her feel good to say it. I guess I ought to take it seriously and enjoy it if he/she is sincere about the feeling.

If someone says something nice about me, then I have to say something nice back.
Who says that this is my responsibility? Why is it? If it is a compliment, then it doesn't have any strings attached, and the only thing that I will want to do is to acknowledge it. Suppose the other person also holds the belief that compliments must be returned? Then he/she would feel obligated to give me a compliment when I returned his/her compliment with one of my own. At that point, I would have to return his/her compliment, and then he/she would have to return mine. This business could go on forever. Neither of us would feel the way we wanted. We probably would feel frustrated with each other, rather than complimentary toward each other. Also, if I struggle to formulate a compliment in return, what does that communicate to the other person?

Counterproductive beliefs about how I should behave or appear to others

If someone gives me a compliment and I accept or agree with it, then people will think that I'm conceited.

Does this belief help me to feel the way I want to feel? No, it doesn't because I would like to feel good about a compliment rather than to feel embarrassed or to worry that others will think that I am conceited. If I am given the compliment, the other person believes that I ought to feel good about myself. Feeling good about oneself is different from boasting and acting conceited. I don't have control over what others think, and constantly worrying about whether they think I am conceited will not stop them from holding that belief if they choose to do so. If they mistake feeling good about being complimented for conceit, that's their problem. Besides, if I worry about appearing conceited when I'm complimented, I'll be inhibited and actually may appear to be aloof and conceited.

EXERCISE MODULE 5
SITUATIONS TO PRACTICE GIVING AND RECEIVING COMPLIMENTS

Giving Compliments

Three situations are provided for you to practice giving compliments. The comments of the other person are not always assertive. However, your task is to be assertive in your comments. In addition, model assertive responses for "you" are given for Situation 1. Remember to practice each situation as many times as you feel it is necessary. Also, use the summary sheet on pages 77-78 when practicing the situations and evaluating your behavior. Finally, you are to design your own situations to practice and develop a list of real-life situations to use as homework assignments.

Situation 1

You have just finished an excellent meal at a friend's home. You want to let your host know how much you enjoyed the dinner. You initiate the first line.

You: _____

Host: They're just some family recipes.

You: _____

Host: It didn't really turn out as I had hoped.

You: _____

Host: Thanks, glad you enjoyed it.

Model Responses for Situation 1

You:	Your dinner was excellent. I enjoyed everything.
Host:	They're just some family recipes.
You:	They are very fine family recipes—especially the vegetable casserole. It was delicious.
Host:	It didn't really turn out as I had hoped.
You:	Well, it all seemed just fine to me. I really enjoyed it all.
Host:	Thanks, glad you enjoyed it.

Situation 2

Your boyfriend/girlfriend/spouse has gone to considerable trouble to rearrange his/her schedule so the two of you could spend a few evenings together. Your boyfriend/girlfriend/spouse knew that this was important for you right now. You want to thank him/her for working out the arrangements.

You: _____

Boy/Girl/Spouse: You would have done the same for me.

You: _____

Boy/Girl/Spouse: Thanks, I'm glad we will have the time together.

chapter 2: Expressing Positive Feelings

Situation 3

You run into a friend you haven't seen in three months. He/she has lost about fifteen pounds and looks terrific. You want to compliment him/her on how good he/she looks. You have both gone through the formalities of "Hi, how are you," and now you want to compliment him/her.

You: _____

Friend: You can't mean me.

You: _____

Friend: I don't know exactly what you mean.

You: _____

Friend: Thanks, I was glad I lost that weight.

Writing Your Own Practice Situations and Deciding on Homework Assignments

After you have practiced the above situations, you can write some personal situations that involve giving compliments. You should develop situations that are likely to occur in your daily interactions and in which you feel you could use some practice. These situations also may be related to the homework assignments that you plan to try out in your environment. Remember, the main point of all the practice is to help you to express yourself in real-life interactions.

On the next two pages, space is provided to develop your own situations to practice. Space is also provided for you to jot down homework assignments.

Exercise Module 5

Personal Situation—Giving a Compliment

Describe Situation: _____
_____
_____

You: _____
_____

Other Person: _____
_____

You: _____
_____

Other Person: _____
_____

You: _____
_____

Personal Situation—Giving a Compliment

Describe Situation: _____
_____
_____

You: _____
_____

Other Person: _____
_____

You: _____
_____

Other Person: _____
_____

You: _____
_____

Homework Assignment

List some possible situations in which you could practice giving compliments when appropriate in your daily interactions. After you complete your list, star * a few you would like to begin with. Choose one for your first assignment in giving compliments. You may find it helpful to rehearse your homework assignments before you try your new behavior in your daily interactions. Remember to start out with easy assignments first, and remember both to evaluate (criteria card in Discussion Module 4) and record (Tables 3 and 4) your behavior.

1.

2.

3.

4.

5.

6.

Receiving Compliments

Three situations are provided for you to practice receiving compliments. The comments of the other person are not always assertive. However, your task is to be assertive in your comments. In addition, model assertive responses for "you" are given for the first situation (Situation 4). Remember to practice each situation as many times as you feel it is necessary. Also, use the summary sheet on pages 77-78 when practicing these situations and in evaluating your behavior. Finally, you are to design your own situations to practice and develop a list of real-life situations to use as homework assignments.

Situation 4

You gave a presentation in class/at a staff meeting/at a PTA meeting yesterday. You know your presentation was good. You spent a lot of time on it and also practiced how to deliver it. A classmate/staff member/acquaintance who heard the speech yesterday is complimenting you.

Classmate/Staff Member/ Acquaintance: Your speech yesterday was very interesting. I really enjoyed it.

You: _____

Classmate/Staff Member/ Acquaintance: You must have done a lot of research on your topic. It was the best presentation this year.

You: _____

chapter 2: Expressing Positive Feelings

Model Responses for Situation 4

Classmate/Staff Member/ Acquaintance:	Your speech yesterday was very interesting. I really enjoyed it.
You:	Thank you. I think it's a really interesting and important area.
Classmate/Staff Member/ Acquaintance:	You must have done a lot of research on your topic. It was the best presentation this year.
You:	I really appreciate your comments. I did spend a lot of time on it.

Situation 5

You took your fourteen-year-old child and his/her friend to a show. Your child's friend comes up to thank you.

Child's Friend:	Mr./Mrs. _____, I really thought it was nice of you to take me to that show yesterday.
You:	_____
Child's Friend:	My mom said to thank you also. She was really glad I could see it.
You:	_____
Child's Friend:	Thanks again.

Exercise Module 5

Situation 6

You are always very thoughtful and never forget your friends' birthdays, anniversaries, and other special occasions. One of your good friends has just called you up on the phone to express his/her appreciation for your thoughtfulness.

Friend: I called to thank you for your card. You always remember my special days. I don't know how you do it.

You: _____
_____

Friend: It is so nice to know someone is thinking about you. I really enjoyed your card.

You: _____
_____

Writing Your Own Practice Situations and Deciding on Homework Assignments

After you have practiced the above situations, you can write some personal situations that involve receiving compliments. You should develop situations that are likely to occur in your daily interactions and in which you feel you could use some practice. These situations also may be related to the homework assignments that you plan to try out in your environment. Remember, the main point of all the practice is to help you to express yourself in real-life interactions.

On the next two pages, space is provided to develop your own situations to practice. Space is also provided to jot down homework assignments.

Personal Situation—Receiving a Compliment

Describe Situation: _____
_____
_____

You: _____
_____

Other Person: _____
_____

You: _____
_____

Other Person: _____
_____

You: _____
_____

Personal Situation—Receiving a Compliment

Describe Situation: _____
_____
_____

You: _____
_____

Other Person: _____
_____

You: _____
_____

Other Person: _____
_____

You: _____
_____

Exercise Module 5

Homework Assignment

List some possible situations in which you could practice receiving a compliment when appropriate in your daily interactions. After you complete your list, star * a few you would like to begin with. Choose one for your first assignment in receiving a compliment. You may find it helpful to rehearse your homework assignments before you try your new behavior in your daily interactions. Remember to start out with easy assignments first, and remember both to evaluate (criteria card in Discussion Module 4) and record (Tables 3 and 4) your behavior.

1.

2

3.

4.

5.

6.

Discussion Module **6**

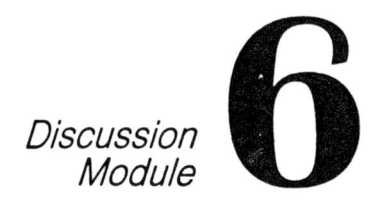

Making Requests

This category, making requests, includes asking for favors, asking for help or assistance, and asking another person to change his/her behavior. We believe that you have both the right to make requests of other people and the responsibility to respect their definitive replies to your requests. People are not self-sufficient. They often require assistance from each other in a variety of daily interactions. As a result, we believe that it is natural and acceptable to make requests of other people (for example, to perform certain tasks, to borrow money or possessions, and so on) with the understanding that they are free to comply with the request, refuse the request, or to postpone a decision on the request with no strings or emotional entanglements involved.

Lest we be misunderstood at this point, we want to state emphatically that we are not suggesting that you indiscriminately make requests of other people. We also suggest that you do not postpone performing tasks until it is no longer possible for you to complete them and then ask someone else to take on your responsibilities. You make a nuisance out of yourself by constantly asking others for unnecessary favors. Such behavior is pushy and shows little concern for the rights of others. However, we do believe that it is quite acceptable to make requests when they are needed.

You have the responsibility to respect a definitive no. Often when we make a request of another person, the other person either does not fully understand the nature of our request or has not decided whether he/she wants to comply with it. As a result, his/her responses are sometimes unclear or not definitive. In such instances, it seems appropriate to restate or clarify the request one or more times. However, at some point, a definitive response usually is forthcoming. If this response is negative, further requests would seem to be inappropriate. They would appear pushy or aggressive and would display little or no concern for the rights of the other person. In such a situation, a single request for the other person to reconsider his/her position may be in order, but no more. Appeals to the other person's sense of fair play, begging, threats, insults, or resorting to statements about the responsibilities of true friends seem manipulative and objectionable.

Some common counterproductive beliefs as well as internal dialogues for disputing them are presented below. Discussion Module 3 contains other suggestions about changing misconceptions and counterproductive attitudes.

Counterproductive beliefs about rights and responsibilities

If I ask for a favor, I am imposing on someone.
What is the evidence for this belief? How am I imposing on someone by asking? I am only imposing if I do not believe that the individual has the freedom to reject my request or if I do not allow him/her to do so. I'm also imposing if I believe the request constitutes an unforgivable inconvenience. If I placed myself in the other person's position, would I consider the request to be an unforgivable inconvenience? Or, is it really quite reasonable? As long as I believe that the other person has the right to say no and as long as I don't make a nuisance of myself, I have the right to ask for favors.

Counterproductive or erroneous beliefs about probable consequences

If I make a request, the other person won't be able to say no even if he/she wants to refuse.
What evidence do I have that most people cannot act in their own best interests? If I am not sure that someone really wants to grant my request, I can always ask him/her if he/she prefers that I ask someone else. If I expect to behave assertively in the area of making requests, I need to assume that people can refuse my requests if they want to do so.

If I ask for help or assistance, the other person should realize that I really need it and should help me out . . . (or else).
Does this belief enable me to achieve my goals and to do so without hurting others? Of course, it doesn't. People are free to grant or refuse my requests. They are not obligated to me. If I believe that they are obligated, it only leads me to try to impose my will on them. Such behavior is aggressive and hurts others. All I can do is ask and indicate why I need and would appreciate their help. Then it's up to them. At most, I can indicate my disappointment with them for not helping, but I can't and should not attempt to force them to do my bidding.

If I ask for and receive a favor, then I will be obligated to the other person. I will be expected to do a favor of equal or greater size in the future, and I don't want this obligation.
Why is this so? A favor is a favor is a favor. It is granted or refused freely. Any sense of obligation I feel is self-imposed. If I feel obligated, it probably is because I believe I should be; because I feel that I was not deserving; or because I think of favors as social requirements which are not given freely. Yes, I may feel grateful to someone who has done a favor for me, and I may be more inclined to do a favor in return for him/her. However, in most instances, obligation was not written into the favor when it was granted.

EXERCISE MODULE 6
SITUATIONS TO PRACTICE MAKING REQUESTS

Three situations are provided for you to practice making requests. The comments of the other person are not always assertive. However, your task is to be assertive in your comments. In addition, model assertive responses for "you" are given for Situation 1. Remember to practice each situation as many times as you feel it is necessary. Also use the summary sheet on pages 77-78 when practicing the situations and evaluating your behavior. Finally, you are to design your own situations to practice and develop a list of real-life situations to use as homework assignments.

Situation 1

You are leaving in a few days for a two-week trip and want to ask your neighbor to water your plants and keep an eye on your house while you are away.

You: _____

Neighbor: I'm afraid I might kill your plants.
You: _____

Neighbor: I would hate for anything to happen and have you feel I was responsible.
You: _____

Neighbor: Okay. I'll do that for you. When are you planning to go?

Reminder: Note that your neighbor was thinking aloud. He/she seemed unsure of the situation. You had to clarify your request. Since your neighbor did not give you a definitive no, it was appropriate to clarify your request and ask again. If you felt your neighbor didn't want to do it, you could ask him/her if he/she was saying no to you. "Sue/Joe, are you saying no, or are you just unsure about what I'm asking you to do?"

Exercise Module 6

Model Responses for Situation 1

You: Joe/Sue, I'm leaving Wednesday for that two-week vacation to Mexico I told you about. I'd appreciate it if you would water my plants and keep an eye on my house for me while I'm away.

Neighbor: I'm afraid I might kill your plants.

You: Don't worry about that. I would really appreciate your help.

Neighbor: I would hate for anything to happen and have you feel I was responsible.

You: I would not hold you responsible. I'd just like to have you water the plants and check that everything looks okay.

Neighbor: Okay. I'll do that for you. When are you planning to go?

Situation 2

You have been assigned to work at the local recreation center on Tuesday nights. However, next Tuesday you have some out-of-town company coming for dinner. You'd like to stay with your company for the entire evening. You will have to ask another recreation worker to switch evenings with you.

You: _____

Tom/Betty: I prefer Thursday nights here.

You: _____

Tom/Betty: Sure, I can manage it this time.

You: _____

chapter 2: Expressing Positive Feelings

Situation 3

You handed in a report to your supervisor/professor last week. The report contained several careless errors which your supervisor/professor noticed and commented on almost immediately. You are now concerned about his/her appraisal of your competence. However, you find that in order to complete your present assignment, you need to ask him/her for some help on the technical aspects of the project.

You: _____

Supervisor/Prof: Well, I'm quite busy now.

You: _____

Supervisor/Prof: I'm sure you can figure it out.

You: _____

Supervisor/Prof: Okay, pull up a chair—let's take a look at it.

Reminder: Supervisors, professors, etc., often encourage their employees and students to handle as much of their assignments on their own as possible. However, if and when you really do need help, they usually will assist. You do have the right to make a request or ask for help from supervisors, professors, etc.

Writing Your Own Practice Situations and Deciding on Homework Assignments

After you have practiced the above situations, you can write some personal situations that involve making requests. You should develop situations that are likely to occur in your daily interactions and in which you feel you could use some practice. These situations also may be related to the homework assignments that you plan to try out in your environment. Remember, the main point of all the practice is to help you to express yourself in real-life interactions.

On the next two pages, space is provided to develop your own situations to practice. Space is also provided for you to jot down homework assignments.

Exercise Module 6

Personal Situation—Making a Request

Describe Situation: _____
_____
_____

You: _____
_____

Other Person: _____
_____

You: _____
_____

Other Person: _____
_____

You: _____
_____

Personal Situation—Making a Request

Describe Situation: _____
_____
_____

You: _____
_____

Other Person: _____
_____

You: _____
_____

Other Person: _____
_____

You: _____
_____

Homework Assignment

List some possible situations in which you could practice making a request when appropriate in your daily interactions. After you complete your list, star * a few you would like to begin with. Choose one for your first assignment in making a request. You may find it helpful to rehearse your homework assignments before you try your new behavior in your daily interactions. Remember to start out with easy assignments first, and remember both to evaluate (criteria card in Discussion Module 4) and record (Tables 3 and 4) your behavior.

1.

2.

3.

4.

5.

6.

Exercise Module 6

Discussion Module **7**

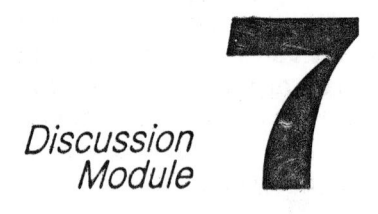

Expressing Liking, Love, and Affection

You have the right to express in an appropriate manner feelings of love, liking, or affection to those for whom you have such feelings. For most people, hearing or receiving such sincere expressions constitutes a most pleasant and meaningful interaction and one which often strengthens and deepens the relationship between the parties. In many cases, failure to express these feelings can result in friction or disruption of close personal relationships. Such an omission can lead the other person to feel taken for granted or unappreciated and can weaken the relationship. Obviously, the appropriateness of the time and the place of expression are important factors in asserting very personal feelings.

It is important to respect the other person's reactions to your feelings. He/she may not reciprocate your feelings, now or in the future, and may not experience these feelings to the extent that you do. You can control only what you feel and say, not what the other person feels or says.

Some misconceptions and counterproductive attitudes which prevent the expression of these feelings as well as internal dialogues for disputing them are presented below. Discussion Module 3 contains additional suggestions about how to change misconceptions and counterproductive beliefs.

Counterproductive beliefs about how I should behave or appear to others

It's too emotional (unmasculine) to express these feelings, and besides I feel silly doing so.

Why is this so? Such feelings are legitimate and healthy. Who says that I'm not supposed to express these feelings? What does masculinity have to do with feeling and expressing love and affection to someone? If I have these feelings and I want to express them, then I can feel free to express them in an appropriate manner.

He/she should know how I feel by now. Why do I have to say it?
What evidence do I have for this belief? Since when have other people become mind readers? I know that a direct expression is subject to less misinterpretation than no expression. People feel unappreciated and taken for granted if they don't hear sincere expressions of how others feel toward them from time to time. If I have these feelings, it's best to express them.

Counterproductive or erroneous beliefs about probable consequences

Expressing love, liking, and affection is risky since the other person may not feel the same way. If he/she doesn't feel the same way, where does that leave me?
This belief certainly does not help me to feel the way I want to feel. If I expect this relationship to become closer, someone will have to take some risks. If the other person doesn't feel the same way, at least I'll know. Wouldn't I rather express how I feel and take my chances than leave the other person and myself in doubt? If the other person doesn't feel the same way, then we can either work on the relationship or develop other more satisfying relationships.

If I tell the other person how I feel, then he/she should tell me how he/she feels . . . (or else).
Does this belief allow me to achieve my goals and to do so without hurting others? No, it doesn't. All I can do is to tell the other person my feelings and ask about his/hers. I can't force the other person to tell me how he/she feels. If I try to do so, I'm certainly violating his/her rights, and I'm probably working against my own best interests.

EXERCISE MODULE 7
SITUATIONS TO PRACTICE EXPRESSING LIKING, LOVE, AND AFFECTION

Three situations are provided for you to practice expressing liking, love, and affection. The comments of the other person are not always assertive. However, your task is to be assertive in your comments. In addition, model assertive responses for "you" are given for Situation 1. Remember to practice each situation as many times as you feel it is necessary. Also use the summary sheet on pages 77-78 when practicing the situations and evaluating your behavior. Finally you, are to design your own situations to practice and develop a list of real-life situations to use as homework assignments.

Situation 1

You have a friend whose friendship you have valued for many years. You have always accepted this relationship and taken it for granted. Now you realize you would like to assert yourself and tell him/her how much he/she means to you.

You: _____

Friend: Me?

You: _____

Friend: I don't know what to say.

You: _____

chapter 2: Expressing Positive Feelings

Model Responses for Situation 1

You: Sue/Sam, I want you to know that I really value your friendship. You're great to be around.
Friend: Me?
You: You always seem to be there, to say the right thing.
Friend: I don't know what to say.
You: You needn't say anything. I just wanted you to know that I like you and I'm glad you're my friend.

Situation 2

You often feel quite affectionate toward your boyfriend/girlfriend/spouse, but rarely express these feelings. You and your boyfriend/girlfriend/spouse are sitting in the living room alone. You want to tell him/her how you feel toward him/her.

You: _____

Boyfriend/Girl/Spouse: Oh!

You: _____

Boyfriend/Girl/Spouse: Well, that's nice to hear.

Exercise Module 7

Situation 3

Your father/mother/father-in-law/mother-in-law are very good to you. They are supportive, but not overbearing. They give suggestions when appropriate, but do not order or command. You feel you're lucky to have such parents/parents-in-law. You want to express your affection toward them.

You: _____

Father/Mother/In-Laws: Anyone in my position would do as I do.

You: _____

Father/Mother/In-Laws: That makes me feel good. I'm really glad you're my son/daughter/son-in-law/daughter-in-law.

Writing Your Own Practice Situations and Deciding on Homework Assignments

After you have practiced the above situations, you can write some personal situations that involve expressing liking, love, and affection. You should develop situations that are likely to occur in your daily interactions and in which you feel you could use some practice. These situations also may be related to the homework assignments that you plan to try out in your environment. Remember, the main point of all the practice is to help you to express yourself in real-life interactions.

On the next two pages, space is provided to develop your own situations to practice. Space is also provided for you to jot down homework assignments.

Personal Situation—Expressing Liking, Love, and Affection

Describe Situation: _____

You: _____

Other Person: _____

You: _____

Other Person: _____

You: _____

Personal Situation—Expressing Liking, Love, and Affection

Describe Situation: _____

You: _____

Other Person: _____

You: _____

Other Person: _____

You: _____

Exercise Module 7

Homework Assignment

List some possible situations in which you could practice expressing liking, love, and affection when appropriate in your daily interactions. After you complete your list, star * a few you would like to begin with. Choose one for your first assignment in expressing liking, love, and affection. You may find it helpful to rehearse your homework assignments before you try your new behavior in your daily interactions. Remember to start out with easy assignments first, and remember both to evaluate (criteria card in Discussion Module 4) and record (Tables 3 and 4) your behavior.

1.

2.

3.

4.

5.

6.

Discussion Module **8**

Initiating and Maintaining Conversations

You have the right to initiate conversations with other people. Most people enjoy meeting others and usually respond favorably to people who attempt to initiate contact with them. On occasion, some people will not welcome such interactions. In these instances, you have the responsibility not to force yourself on them. Unfortunately, it is not immediately clear whether an individual is unwilling to engage in a conversation or whether he/she is initially shy or distrustful. After a few comments, such a differentiation often can be made. Unwillingness to engage in social interactions is sometimes indicated by: lack of smiles, hostile looks or comments, unresponsive nonverbal behavior, curt responses, and failure to ask the initiator questions in return. Conversely, willingness to engage in social interaction is indicated by: frequent smiles and gestures which indicate nonverbal responsiveness, verbal responses which disclose personal information, and/or questions directed to the initiator.

Many people report difficulty in knowing when to initiate a conversation and how to do it. It usually is easier to begin a conversation if you have the other person's attention and if you are not more than a few feet away so that you can be heard easily. Once you catch the other person's eye, you can smile and say whatever it is that you would like to say. In most initial conversations, people search for a topic of common interest to break the ice, for example, "I notice you are reading _____. Are you in Dr. Frederick's English class?" or "Hi, I'm Bill Smith and I work in production. I've seen you around here lately, and I was wondering in which department you work."

Once a common topic has been established, there are several ways of maintaining and expanding the conversation. One way is to make a statement and then ask the other person for his/her views on the matter. Another way is to disclose personally relevant information such as likes, dislikes, attitudes, and so on. It is important that what you disclose be relevant to the topic and not be so personal that it seems out of place. Most people do not divulge their deepest secrets to total strangers. The idea is to make your comments gradually a little more personal so that the conversation becomes more meaningful. Another procedure is not to answer questions with a simple yes or no, but to give your answer and perhaps explain your views, so that the other person has something to which he/she can respond. Also, asking questions which require more than a simple yes or no answer is helpful. Instead of asking, "Do you like Smith, the guy running for mayor?" you can say, "What do you think of Smith's views?" The second question encourages more participation in the conversation than the first question.

We suggest that you do not rely solely on one of these procedures to the exclusion of the others, since this can result in a mechanical or stilted conversation (like conversations in which you only ask the other person a series of questions). Rather, your goal is to integrate these procedures so that the conversation flows smoothly. At first, you may find that you are self-conscious, but this feeling will be reduced over time as you practice your skills.

Listed below are some of the common counterproductive attitudes that block attempts to initiate social interaction. We have provided internal dialogues for disputing them, and we refer you to Discussion Module 3 for additional procedures for disputing such attitudes.

Counterproductive beliefs about rights and responsibilities

I don't have the right to impose on or bother other people.

What evidence do I have that initiating a conversation and trying to be friendly is equivalent to imposing on or bothering other people? Most people enjoy meeting others. If they feel that I am bothering them, they will probably indicate this to me in one way or another. Besides, am I afraid of bothering them or of being rejected by them? If I want to start a conversation with someone, I should be able to do so.

But he/she is so important that someone like me can't just go up and start a conversation. It's not right.

Here is another belief that does not help me to feel the way I want to feel. He/she puts on his/her slacks the same way I do and has the same needs that I have. Who knows, perhaps the fact that he/she is so important intimidates people and makes it unlikely that he/she has very many friendly conversations with other people. Maybe I'm doing him/her a favor by beginning a friendly conversation.

Counterproductive beliefs about how I should behave or appear to others

I don't know what to say. If I don't say something brilliant, the other person will think that I'm an idiot, and I should be a brilliant conversationalist.

Well, this belief certainly doesn't help me to feel the way I want to feel. It prevents me from meeting new people. When I think about the topics of most conversations, I realize that they are not about such profound issues. People talk about the weather, TV shows, class, other people, and so on. I can discuss those issues, too. Perhaps what I say is not as important as is clearly indicating my interest in making contact with the other person. If the other person thinks that I'm an idiot, that's his/her problem. At least I'm brave enough to try to meet someone new.

Counterproductive or erroneous beliefs about probable consequences

It's risky to start conversations and, besides, the other person may not like me.

Once again, I've discovered a belief that doesn't help me to feel the way I want to feel. I can't be liked by everyone. If I don't say anything, I minimize the short-run risk of saying something for which I may not be liked; however, I also increase the likelihood of the long-run consequences of having few friends and therefore not having anyone to like me. It's a matter of probabilities. The more conversations I initiate, the more chances I have for meeting new friends. So what if it doesn't work out this time? If I keep trying, some of my attempts will prove very satisfying.

EXERCISE MODULE 8
SITUATIONS TO PRACTICE INITIATING AND MAINTAINING CONVERSATIONS

Six situations are provided for you to practice initiating and maintaining conversations. When you have difficulty initiating a conversation, you need an opening line to get started, whereas, in maintaining a conversation, you need to go beyond the opening line stage. In this module, you will practice both skills. To practice making opening lines, three situations are provided. For each, you should practice a few different ways you could begin the conversation. We have also included two possible opening lines for each of these situations. Practice these opening lines as many times as you feel it is necessary. Use the summary sheet on pages 77-78 to evaluate your behavior. Finally, you are to design your own situations to practice and develop a list of real-life situations to use as homework assignments.

Initiating a Conversation

Situation 1

You are at a party and you do not know anyone but the host/hostess. Practice making some opening lines in order to introduce yourself to someone at the party.

Possible openers

You: _____

or _____

You: _____

_____

Model Responses as Openers

You: Hi, I'm Joe/Jane. I'm a friend of Dick's. I don't know many people here. What's your name?

or

You: I'm Sue/Sam. I don't think I've met you before.

chapter 2: Expressing Positive Feelings

Situation 2

You are sitting with some friends watching a movie on television. You really enjoyed the show and want to know what your friends thought about it. Practice possible opening lines to begin a conversation.

Possible Openers

You: _____

or

You: _____

Model Responses for Situation 2

You: What did you think about the movie?

or

You: I really enjoyed the movie. It reminded me of our high-school days. Did you react to it in that way?

Situation 3

You are with a group of friends now. You are having a good time, but in the back of your mind you are thinking about next Saturday. You would like to suggest that next Saturday the group goes bowling. You usually wait for someone else to make a suggestion, but you decide you will initiate this conversation today.

Possible Openers

You: _____

or

You: _____

Model Responses for Situation 3

You: For next week, I'd like to suggest that we all go bowling.

or

You: We haven't gone bowling in a long time. How do you all feel about bowling for next Saturday?

Exercise Module 8

Maintaining the Conversation

When you begin to work on initiating and maintaining conversations, it may be helpful to list topics you would be interested in talking about. You may also list where you could find interesting topics to discuss. For instance, you could skim a newspaper and locate an article on a community concern. Next, you could think about how you feel on this topic. After you do this, it would be easier to initiate a conversation on this topic and to maintain the conversation as you include your personal opinions and ask for the other person's ideas.

At this point, stop and follow these steps:

Get a newspaper _____
(Paper, Date)

Locate an article of concern_____
(Title of Article)

Write down your feelings on this topic:
_____
_____
_____

Situation 4

Now try a conversation on this article:

You: _____
_____

Person: It's an important concern—I'm not sure how I feel about it.

You: _____
_____

Person: I didn't know you were interested in that.

You: _____
_____

chapter 2: Expressing Positive Feelings

Situation 5

If you are interested in gardening, you may read a little about it. Then you could approach one of your neighbors who obviously spends a lot of time in his/her yard and discuss gardening.

You: _____

Neighbor: I really enjoy being outside.

You: _____

Neighbor: I've been doing this for many years.

You: _____

Neighbor: It does take a lot of work.

You: _____

Situation 6

Think about a movie you've seen, a show you've gone to, or a new store or shopping mall you've visited. You can initiate the conversation by just mentioning you've been to this place or show and then maintain the conversation by discussing the movie/show/shop with the other person.

You: _____

Friend: I've been to it also.

You: _____

Friend: It wasn't what I expected.

You: _____

Friend: Next time you're going, let me know. Perhaps we can go together.

Exercise Module 8

Writing Your Own Practice Situations and Deciding on Homework Assignments

After you have practiced the above situations, you can write some personal situations which involve initiating and maintaining conversations. You should develop situations which are likely to occur in your daily interactions and in which you feel you could use some practice. These situations also may be related to the homework assignments that you plan to try out in your environment. Remember, the main point of all the practice is to help you to express yourself in real-life interactions.

On the next two pages, space is provided to develop your own situations to practice. Space is also provided to jot down homework assignments.

Personal Situation—Initiating and Maintaining Conversations

Describe Situation: _____
_____
_____

You: _____
_____

Other Person: _____
_____

You: _____
_____

Other Person: _____
_____

You: _____
_____

Personal Situation—Initiating and Maintaining Conversations

Describe Situation: _____
_____
_____

You: _____
_____

Other Person: _____
_____

You: _____
_____

Other Person: _____
_____

You: _____
_____

Exercise Module 8

Homework Assignment

List some possible topics in which you could practice initiating and maintaining conversations in your daily interactions. After you complete your list, star * a few topics you would like to begin with. Choose one for your first assignment. You may find it helpful to rehearse your homework assignments before you try your new behavior in your daily interactions. Remember to start out with topics you feel most comfortable with first, and remember both to evaluate (criteria card in Discussion Module 4) and record (Tables 3 and 4) your behavior.

1.

2.

3.

4.

5.

6.

chapter 2: Expressing Positive Feelings

Chapter 3

Self-Affirmation

Within the category of self-affirmation, we have included three behaviors: expressing legitimate rights, refusing requests, and expressing personal opinions including disagreement. An inability to express these behaviors can result in the denial of one's rights and one's self; whereas being able to express these behaviors affirms one's position with respect to the other person.

A general caution is in order with respect to the behaviors in this chapter. Since all of these behaviors are concerned with stating or affirming one's position, point of view, or rights, it is possible for people to become overly zealous when they feel that their rights are being violated or ignored. In addition to being inappropriate, an overly zealous response can lead to aggressive interactions. The objective in all cases is to assert your position firmly, recognizing that the other person usually will respect it. The objective is not to beat the other person over the head with demands or force recognition and compliance with your rights at any price.

As we have mentioned previously, asserting yourself with respect to the behaviors in this chapter, at times, may result in negative reactions from others, particularly if these individuals have been taking advantage of you in the past. On occasion, other people might become impatient, hostile, angry, critical, silent, or sarcastic toward you when you express the above behaviors. If you express yourself in an appropriate manner, these reactions generally do not occur. Nevertheless, you should recognize that unfavorable reactions can occur, and you need to be able to deal with them.

The best way to deal with negative reactions is to minimize the likelihood of their occurrence. In learning to behave assertively, you are changing your customary pattern of interacting with people in your environment. If you explain to the important people in your life (spouse, parents, close friends, and so on) what you are trying to accomplish through self-assertion and enlist their help, you minimize the likelihood that they will react negatively toward you when you try out your new behavior.

There are several ways to deal with negative reactions when they do occur. First, examine your own behavior. Was it appropriate? Did you consider the other person's rights as well as your own? How did you deliver your message? Were you aggressive? If you decide that your behavior was either inappropriate or untimely, then an apology is in order. Following the apology, you can express your position in a more appropriate manner.

A second approach is to ask the other person for clarification about the aspects of your behavior that are disturbing him/her. Based on the information you receive, you can decide whether your behavior or his/her behavior was inappropriate. If you believe that you behaved appropriately and you are satisfied with your behavior, then you may want to restate your position. Restating your position can help to clarify it to the party or parties in case it was misunderstood. Restating your position also indicates that you do not intend to back down in the face of the other person's inappropriate behavior.

The third approach is relevant for those instances in which you appropriately assert yourself, restate, and clarify your position, and yet the other party still reacts unfavorably toward you. At these times, the best way to cope with the reactions may be to ignore them. By ignoring the reactions, you assume that attending to this person's anger or other negative reactions only serves to increase these reactions. Asserting yourself does not involve making an issue of each and every situation merely for the sake of self-affirmation. Once you have stated your point clearly, you need not belabor it.

Discussion Module **9**

Standing Up for Your Legitimate Rights

This category, expressing legitimate rights, is relevant to a variety of situations in which your personal rights are ignored or violated. Some examples of these situations include: consumer situations such as being short-changed, being sold defective merchandise, being served unsatisfactory food in a restaurant, and receiving discourteous or inferior service; parent and family situations such as not being allowed to run your own life and make your own decisions, not having a right to your privacy, and not being allowed to raise your children in your own way; authority situations in which unfair decisions are made about your fate; and friendship situations in which your right to make decisions is not respected.

The question of what one's legitimate personal rights are in a situation is is not always resolved easily. However, we believe that the list of rights provided below constitutes a set of guidelines which will be helpful to people in most situations. The majority of situations which call for you to express your legitimate rights involve the issues raised in personal rights one and two, being fairly treated as a person of worth and being able to make your own decisions. Rights three and four, on the other hand, are relevant to the more restricted, but frequent, set of situations in which you need to express your special rights as a consumer. It is our concern that these rights are not followed blindly, but are used in conjunction with good judgment in each situation.

1. You have the right to be treated fairly and as a person of worth with the same rights, privileges, and responsibilities as everyone else regardless of sex, race, religion, education, profession, social and economic status, etc.

We believe that all men/women are created equal in the sense that they are entitled to similar treatment, rights, and privileges, and have similar responsibilities. The use of special group status or membership to increase the rights and privileges of one person and decrease the rights of another seems totally inappropriate.

2. You have the right to make your own decisions and to live your own life as you choose (as long as you don't hurt other people or violate their rights).

Once an individual reaches adulthood, he/she has the right to make all decisions that will affect his/her life even if such decisions are foolish or in error. It is frequently the case that our rights are violated by people who assume the power to make decisions "in our own best interests." During childhood, such decision-making on the part of parents or significant others may have been appropriate, but, it does not seem appropriate for the overwhelming majority of adults.

3. You have the right to get what you pay for, regardless of how meager the price.

If you purchase an item, that item should be satisfactory or acceptable in every way to you regardless of whether it is a Big Mac from McDonald's or a $250,000 mansion. Our interest is not to encourage picky, unreasonable consumers. Rather, we are concerned that you are able to buy the product as advertised and that you are able to return it if it is defective or unsatisfactory. If it causes an inconvenience for the salesclerk or repairman/woman, that is not and should not be your problem. You are paying for this service.

4. You have the right to prompt and courteous service.

You are paying for service, and you have the right to receive it (not to *demand* it). You do not have to feel guilty for expecting a reasonable amount of the salesperson's, waiter/waitress's, or repairman/woman's time and attention.

Once you are aware of your rights, it is easier to recognize situations in which they are being violated and which call for you to assert yourself. In Discussion Module 3, we discussed some of the cues by which you can recognize whether an assertion may be needed. You may want to review this material. In general, if you are unsure of whether your rights are being violated, you may find it helpful to ask yourself two questions: "Am I being treated fairly and as a person of worth regardless of sex, etc?" and "Am I being deprived of my right to make my own decisions?" Being able to stand up for one's rights is important because it affirms one's self and one's sense of being able to influence one's life and circumstances.

In expressing or standing up for legitimate rights, there is an extreme behavior which should be avoided. It is exemplified by the person who is now aware and sensitive (oversensitive?) to his/her rights and zealously crusades to stand up for each and every right that is violated because of the principle involved. Obviously, such behavior can be aggressive and obnoxious. The important point is to stand up for your rights in situations in which they are violated and in which it is objectionable to you that the violation has occurred.

There are risks involved when you express your legitimate rights. It is important to be aware of these risks and to weigh them prior to choosing your course of action. The most common risk is that, when you stand up for your legitimate rights, people, particularly those who have taken advantage of your failure to do so in the past, may not like your new behavior. We believe that it generally is more desirable to stand up for your rights in an assertive manner, feel good about yourself, and take the possible risk than it is to squelch your feelings and self-esteem in order to avoid risking the good will of others. You will find that many people will respect you for your position.

There are situations in which standing up for legitimate rights that clearly have been violated is inadvisable. Such situations are rare, but they include instances in which physical abuse or legal penalties are likely to be forthcoming. For example, if you are deliberately crowded off the sidewalk by a group of tough-looking individuals, or if you are being given an unfair citation by a very angry or hostile policeman, you probably will want to choose not to stand up for your rights at the time of the situation. Both of these situations are unusual, but they point out the importance of the need for brief but considered judgment before you act.

Some counterproductive beliefs concerning standing up for your rights and internal dialogues for disputing these beliefs are presented below. Discussion Module 3 contains additional suggestions which you may want to review.

Counterproductive beliefs about rights and responsibilities

I know my rights are being violated. This pizza isn't the way I ordered it, but I really don't care that much.

Does the belief help me to avoid significant unpleasantness without denying my rights? No. If I don't care about having my rights violated, then there is no reason to assert myself. However, I don't like anchovies on my pizza, and I don't like having to pick them off. So, why am I trying to talk myself into not caring when I really do care? I have the right to get what I pay for and to assert myself about this matter even if it causes the waiter/waitress inconvenience. Maybe it does make me a little nervous to ask for another pizza. It's really no big deal when I compare it to how annoyed I'm going to feel if I accept this one. As long as I do it assertively, I can ask for another pizza.

I don't have the right to reevaluate my position and to change it. If I do change my position, I should apologize and provide an elaborate justification to all concerned.

Does this belief help me to feel the way I want to feel? No. At times, I make decisions hastily or I see the issue in a different way at a later time. If I adhere to my earlier position, I will be unhappy with myself. Of course, I don't want to make a habit of saying one thing on one day and something different on another day. People won't appreciate that type of behavior. However, if I take a position on an issue or make a decision and later feel differently about it, I do have the right to revise my position without having to apologize for the revision. I have the right to change my mind.

I don't have the right to terminate a conversation. I have to listen to the other person for as long as he/she wishes to speak.

Why is this belief true? What evidence supports it? I do not have to engage in a conversation if this is not what I want. Do I have to remain in a conversation if I have something else to do or if I do not want to continue discussing the topic at hand? No, I have the right simply to tell the other person either, "I have to go now. I have something to attend to," or "I'd like to discontinue this conversation. I do not want to discuss that subject any more."

Counterproductive beliefs about how I should behave or appear to others

I don't want to appear demanding and unreasonable about the matter. People shouldn't act that way.

Does this belief help me to feel the way I want to feel? If I feel that my rights are violated and I'm not happy about the situation, then I have the right to say something about it even if the other person thinks I'm demanding. I have two choices. On the one hand, I can assert myself and take the chance of being thought of as demanding. On the other hand, I can say nothing and remain dissatisfied with the situation. If I am assertive, the chances are that he/she won't really think I'm demanding.

Counterproductive or erroneous beliefs about probable consequences

If I stand up for my rights, the other person won't like me so I'd better not risk it.

Does this belief help me to feel the way I want to feel? I know that there are risks involved. Some people won't like me if I stand up for my rights, particularly if they have been taking advantage of me in the past. However, my self-esteem is more important than their goodwill. I'll express my rights and feel good about it, and let the chips fall where they may. I can always make new acquaintances if it comes down to that. Besides, what kind of a relationship is it when my rights often are violated?

I'm a human being with rights just like everyone else. People should respect my rights . . . (or else).

Does this belief help me to achieve my goals and to do so without hurting others? I do have rights, and I can speak up when they are being violated. But I don't have the right to secure my rights at any cost. I can only assert my rights. I don't have the right to force other people to comply with them.

EXERCISE MODULE 9
SITUATIONS TO PRACTICE STANDING UP
FOR YOUR LEGITIMATE RIGHTS

Four situations are provided for you to practice standing up for your legitimate rights. The comments of the other person are not always assertive. However, your task is to be assertive in your comments. In addition, model assertive responses for "you" are given for Situation 1. Remember to practice each situation as many times as you feel it is necessary. Also use the summary sheet on pages 77-78 when practicing the situations and evaluating your behavior. Finally, you are to design your own situations to practice and develop a list of real-life situations to use as homework assignments.

Situation 1

You've gone to lunch at a restaurant. You've ordered a chef's salad with Thousand Island dressing. However, when you get your salad it has blue cheese dressing on it. You prefer Thousand Island. The waiter/waitress is approaching your area now.

Waiter/Waitress: Is everything okay?
You: _____
_____

Waiter/Waitress: I distinctly remember you ordering blue cheese dressing.
You: _____
_____

Waiter/Waitress: I have it written down right here on my slip—blue cheese.
You: _____
_____

Waiter/Waitress: All right, I'll be back in a few minutes.

Reminder: Don't get sidetracked into arguing who is right. You need not attack the waiter/waitress' competence. Just repeat what you'd like.

Model Responses for Situation 1

Waiter/Waitress: Is everything okay?
You: No. I ordered my salad with Thousand Island dressing and it came with blue cheese. I'd like you to return this one and bring me a salad with Thousand Island dressing.
Waiter/Waitress: I distinctly remember you ordering blue cheese dressing.
You: I believe I ordered Thousand Island and I'd appreciate your exchanging this salad.
Waiter/Waitress: I have it written down right here on my slip—blue cheese.
You: There's been a mistake. I'd like a salad with Thousand Island dressing.
Waiter/Waitress: All right, I'll be back in a few minutes.

Situation 2

Your dentist's receptionist calls you and asks you to cancel your appointment because too many patients were scheduled for the same time. You made your appointment at least a month ago and feel you have a right to see the dentist tomorrow.

Receptionist: Hello _____. This is Ms. Jones at Dr. Lake's office. We'd like to cancel your appointment tomorrow. We overscheduled for the afternoon.

You: _____

Receptionist: We just have too many people for the afternoon. I'd like to reschedule you for three weeks from today.

You: _____

Receptionist: Yes, you did schedule your appointment a long time back.

You: _____

Receptionist: I see what you mean. We'll see you tomorrow at 3 P.M.

Reminder: You have a right to your scheduled appointment unless an emergency situation arises. Remember, if you had missed your appointment, you may well have been charged for the time. Your time is also important.

Situation 3

You have been dieting for weeks and have managed to take off a few pounds. You go to a friend's house for a dinner party and he/she absolutely insists you try some of everything and have doubles.

Friend: Have some of this.

You: _____

Friend: Oh, diets don't count on Saturday night.

You: _____

Friend: But you've lost so much weight, a little nibble won't hurt.

You: _____

Friend: This cheese cake is my specialty. It takes twelve eggs and two hours to make, not to mention one pound of cream cheese.

You: _____

Friend: Just try the homemade bread. It's worth every calorie.

You: _____

Friend: I guess you are pretty serious about your diet. I am glad that you did come tonight, even if you can't partake of it all.

Reminder: You do not have to eat everything. You did not tell your friend to spend all day cooking. You are not responsible for how she/he uses her/his time. You need not be made to feel guilty for not tasting everything.

Exercise Module 9

Situation 4

You've just received a note from your parents/friend/relatives indicating that they are coming to visit next weekend. You have plans for this weekend already and do not want company. You call your parents/friend/relatives to tell them it has to be another time.

Parents/Friend/Relatives: Hi _____. We can't wait to see you.

You: _____
_____

Parents/Friend/Relatives: Well, we've made all our plans already.

You: _____
_____

Parents/Friend/Relatives: We'd have a great time. We wouldn't be in the way.

You: _____
_____

Parents/Friend/Relatives: Okay—I'll call you tomorrow to check on another time.

Writing Your Own Practice Situations and Deciding on Homework Assignments

After you have practiced the above situations, you can write some personal situations that involve standing up for your legitimate rights. You should develop situations that are likely to occur in your daily interactions and in which you feel you could use some practice. These situations also may be related to the homework assignments that you plan to try out in your environment. Remember, the main point of all the practice is to help you to express yourself in real-life interactions.

On the next two pages, space is provided to develop your own situations to practice. Space is also provided for you to jot down homework assignments.

Personal Situation—Standing Up for Your Legitimate Rights

Describe Situation: _____
_____
_____

You: _____
_____

Other Person: _____
_____

You: _____
_____

Other Person: _____
_____

You: _____
_____

Personal Situation—Standing Up for Your Legitimate Rights

Describe Situation: _____
_____
_____

You: _____
_____

Other Person: _____
_____

You: _____
_____

Other Person: _____
_____

You: _____
_____

Exercise Module 9

Homework Assignment

List some possible situations in which you could practice standing up for your legitimate rights when appropriate in your daily interactions. After you complete your list, star * a few you would like to begin with. Choose one for your first assignment in standing up for your legitimate rights. You may find it helpful to rehearse your homework assignments before you try your new behavior in your daily interactions. Remember to start out with easy assignments first, and remember both to evaluate (criteria card in Discussion Module 4) and record (Tables 3 and 4) your behavior.

1.

2.

3.

4.

5.

6.

Discussion Module

10

Refusing Requests

You have the right to say no to requests that are unreasonable and to re-quests which, although reasonable, you do not care to grant. Being able to say no when you mean no is important for a variety of reasons. First, it helps you to avoid becoming involved in situations which you think you will regret being involved in at a later time. It also helps to prevent the development of circumstances in which you will feel as though you have been taken advantage of, abused, or manipulated into doing something which you did not care to do. Finally, it allows you, rather than the other person, to make your decisions and to direct your life in that situation.

There are several points that are important to be aware of in situations in which requests are made of you. First, when someone makes a request, they are asking you to do something for them. It is their perfect right to make such a request. However, a request is something which you are perfectly free to grant or reject. It is not a social or moral obligation with emotional strings attached to it. Therefore, there is no reason to feel guilty or devoid of humanitarian spirit if you do not grant the request. Any attempt by the other person to manipulate you into granting it by making you feel uncomfortable is inappropriate and needs to be resisted. You may want to consult Discussion Module 6, Making Requests, for additional comments on this point and on related issues.

Be sure you completely understand the request before you make your decision. If you don't understand it, ask for clarification and, if necessary, repeated clarification until you do understand it. Often it is those vague, small, or innocent requests which turn out to have those hidden, objectionable commitments or fine print buried in them. You have the right to understand what is being asked of you before you make your decision. Moreover, some people will attempt to capitalize on your fear of appearing unintelligent if you have to ask for clarification. The result is that you are pushed into making decisions that may not be in your best interests.

You also have the right to postpone making a decision. If you are not sure about how you feel about a decision, it is appropriate and even desirable to postpone a decision on the matter. In postponing the decision, you need not feel compelled to give a time or date by which you will make the decision. Our intent is not to encourage you to postpone making a decision because you are afraid that you will have to say no to someone. Rather, we are concerned with those situations in which you feel pressured to make a hasty and premature decision. For example, a common principle of selling is to get the customer to make a decision on an article of merchandise while he/she is with the salesperson and before he/she has an opportunity to do some comparison shopping or to evaluate the decision carefully and change his/her mind.

When you have decided to refuse a request, say no definitively and, if necessary, repeatedly. If you give excuses or long-winded explanations for your behavior, the other person may point out the lack of logic and the weaknesses in your arguments, thereby disarming you and resulting in your feeling had. You need not feel responsible for justifying your refusal. If you feel pushed in the situation, you can always say something such as, "I just don't want to do it, so I would appreciate it if you wouldn't ask me again. My answer will remain the same." When your answers aren't definitive, you communicate to the other person that he/she has not convinced you yet and thereby reinforce his/her repeating the request. Once you have given a definitive response, further requests by the other person would seem pushy and inappropriate and can be ignored.

Listed below are some common counterproductive attitudes about refusing requests as well as internal dialogues to dispute them. You may want to refer to Discussion Module 3 for additional suggestions about changing counterproductive attitudes.

Counterproductive beliefs about rights and responsibilities

It's such a worthy cause (reasonable request). It's not right to refuse.

Why is this so? Can I support all the worthy causes and grant all the reasonable requests with which I am confronted? Of course not. It's up to me to decide for myself what causes I'll support and what requests I'll grant. Just because it is reasonable or worthy is not sufficient. I have the right to say no if that's the way I feel. I don't have to justify my decision or to refute the other person's rationale.

Counterproductive beliefs about how I should behave or appear to others

After he/she has shown me so many of these items, it would be cruel and insensitive to him/her not to buy at least one.

Why is this so? I came in with the idea of buying something if there was something I liked. I didn't come in to give this salesperson a hard time. Besides, he/she is getting paid and should realize that he/she can't make every sale. There is no reason for me to feel guilty, because I haven't done anything that is unfair or insensitive. If I appreciate his/her service, then I can say so. However, I am free to refuse to buy any items if they are not what I want.

If I really am a friend, I should grant that request.

Why is this so? Does friendship mean that I have to grant requests each and every time they are made? Does it mean having someone else make my decisions for me? Of course not. Certainly, I feel more inclined to do a favor for a friend than for a stranger, but my friendship shouldn't hinge on that. If this other person is really my friend, he/she will understand and respect my decision not to grant this request.

Counterproductive or erroneous beliefs about probable consequences

It is easier to grant this person's request than to face how he/she will feel if I don't grant it.
This belief certainly doesn't help me to feel the way I want to feel or to avoid significant unpleasantness. This person just keeps asking and asking, and it's unpleasant each time it happens. Maybe I'm just encouraging him/her to ask me since he/she knows that I won't refuse. Right now I'm avoiding what I think will be an unpleasant experience if I say no, but as a result I have to endure a lot of unpleasant feelings each time I say yes. I have the right to say no. Perhaps if I say it in a definitive, assertive way, he/she won't bother me about it again. I'm not really sure that he/she will be upset if I say no. It's not my responsibility to sacrifice myself for his/her requests. It is my right to refuse if I want to refuse.

EXERCISE MODULE 10
SITUATIONS TO PRACTICE REFUSING REQUESTS

Three situations are provided for you to practice refusing requests. The comments of the other person are not always assertive. However, your task is to be assertive in your comments. In addition, model assertive responses for "you" are given for Situation 1. Remember to practice each situation as many times as you feel it is necessary. Also use the summary sheet on pages 77-78 when practicing the situations and evaluating your behavior. Finally, you are to design your own situations to practice and develop a list of real-life situations to use as homework assignments.

Situation 1

A mooching friend at work/school keeps borrowing 50¢, 25¢, 5¢, for one thing or another—a soda, a sandwich, the parking meter, etc. He/she never pays you back, although he/she owes you at least $6 by now. Until he/she pays you back, you don't want to give him/her any more money. You have plenty of money, including *change* in your pocket/purse. Here comes your friend now.

Moocher: Hey, I don't have any money and I want to get a snack in the cafeteria. How about loaning me 50¢?

You: _____

Moocher: I'll pay you back.

You: _____

Moocher: You don't trust me—that's great.

You: _____

Moocher: I'd lend it to you if you asked me.

You: _____

Moocher: You're really cheap. How about a quarter then?

You: _____

Moocher: See ya around.

Reminder: It is not necessary to make up excuses—"I don't have any change," "I'm short on money," or preach to the moocher, "You should not always borrow money," "You should work for your own money," etc.

Model Responses for Situation 1

Moocher: Hey, I don't have any money and I want to get a snack in the cafeteria. How about loaning me 50¢?

You: No Jean/John. I don't intend to loan you any more money until you pay me back what you already owe me.

Moocher: I'll pay you back.

You: No more loans until you do.

Moocher: You don't trust me—that's great.

You: The point is you already owe me $6.

Moocher: I'd lend it to you if you asked me.

You: Perhaps, but I want my $6 repaid before I loan you any more.

Moocher: You're really cheap. How about a quarter then?

You: No. No more loans until I get my $6.

Moocher: See ya around.

Reminder: "You" simply repeated your message a number of times until the moocher understood "no more loans until I'm repaid."

Situation 2

You and your boyfriend/girlfriend/spouse have been planning a quiet evening for several days. Another couple stops by and asks you to join them for dinner.

Friend: How about joining us for dinner?

You: _____

Friend: We would really love to have you come.

You: _____

Friend: We will be so disappointed if you don't come. You know how much we enjoy your company.

You: _____

Friend: Dinner is already planned—shrimp casserole, salad, and baked Alaska for dessert. You know how much trouble that all takes.

You: _____

Friend: We haven't seen you in so long that I'm beginning to wonder if we've done something to offend you.

You: _____

Friend: I can really understand that the two of you want to be alone. Let's make it another time.

Reminder: You have a right to spend a quiet evening at home. You need not feel guilty that your friends planned a fancy dinner. You never told them you were coming for dinner.

Situation 3

A very persistent magazine salesman has come to your door. He is asking you to help him "gain some points," and if he gets enough points, he will be able to go to college for a semester. The young salesman gains his points, obviously, by selling magazines, but his pitch is aimed in large part at "people like you who are helping me work my way through college." You are not at all interested in buying a subscription to a magazine.

Salesman: Good afternoon. I'm working my way through college with the help of many kind people like yourself. I need to have 500 points by tonight to go to school for a semester, and right now I have 470. Could I talk to you about how you could help me get the points I need?

You: _____

Salesman: I have a number of fine magazines here, and I'm sure you'll find some you'd like to have.

You: _____

Salesman: Even if you don't want any personally, magazine subscriptions make excellent gifts for your family and friends, or you could send a subscription to a Veteran's Hospital. Just last month I gave a friend a subscription to *Sports Afield* for his birthday. I only need two more subscriptions to go to college this fall.

You: _____

Writing Your Own Practice Situations and Deciding on Homework Assignments

After you have practiced the above situations, you can write some personal situations that involve refusing requests. You should develop situations that are likely to occur in your daily interactions and in which you feel you could use some practice. These situations also may be related to the homework assignments that you plan to try out in your environment. Remember, the main point of all the practice is to help you to express yourself in real-life interactions.

On the next two pages, space is provided to develop your own situations to practice. Space is also provided to jot down homework assignments.

Exercise Module 10

Personal Situation—Refusing Requests

Describe Situation: _____
_____
_____

You: _____
_____

Other Person: _____
_____

You: _____
_____

Other Person: _____
_____

You: _____
_____

Personal Situation—Refusing Requests

Describe Situation: _____
_____
_____

You: _____
_____

Other Person: _____
_____

You: _____
_____

Other Person: _____
_____

You: _____
_____

Homework Assignment

List some possible situations in which you could practice refusing requests when appropriate in your daily interactions. After you complete your list, star * a few you would like to begin with. Choose one for your first assignment in refusing requests. You may find it helpful to rehearse your homework assignments before you try your new behavior in your daily interactions. Remember to start out with easy assignments first, and remember both to evaluate (criteria card in Discussion Module 4) and record (Tables 3 and 4) your behavior.

1.

2.

3.

4.

5.

6.

Discussion Module **11**

Expressing Personal Opinions

You have the right to express your personal opinions assertively. However, you do not have the right to force other people to accept those opinions or even to listen to them. The personal opinion category is rather broad, and in some ways expressing personal opinions is fundamental to all of the assertive behavior categories. Expressing personal opinions is concerned with volunteering a personal preference or taking a stand on an issue. It also includes being able to express an opinion which is in disagreement or potential disagreement with that of another person. Some examples of situations which call for you to express your personal opinions include: deciding how to spend an evening; choosing the color of a new car; expressing your opinions about friends; discussing a political issue; and expressing disagreement with another person's point of view. Each of these situations could involve one or more people and might require you to initiate the conversation, to volunteer an opinion, or to respond to a preceding question or point of view. All of the situations offer you an opportunity to express your opinions.

Of course, we hope that you will choose freely to express or withhold your opinions in accordance with your evaluation of what is appropriate in that situation. We are concerned that you be able to express your opinions if you want to and that you do not feel pressured to adopt, to agree with, or to voice an opinion which runs counter to your own. We believe that people generally feel better about themselves if they are able to say what they think rather than being excessively concerned or preoccupied by anxiety about expressing themselves.

When you express your opinions, it is important to state them definitively and firmly. However, it is a violation of other people's rights if you badger or force them to accept or listen to your opinions when they clearly indicate that they are not interested.

Of course, there are potential risks that are involved in stating one's opinions, and you should be aware of them when you decide whether to express yourself in a given situation. One of the most common risks is that some people won't agree with your opinions. Others, of course, will. It is perhaps not as important that people agree with your opinions as it is to be able to express those opinions appropriately and to feel good about being able to do so. It is possible that some people might become angry or penalize you in some way for your opinions. Such occurrences probably are more infrequent than we fear; however, they do occur. If risk is realistic in a given situation, then it should be taken into account when you decide whether to assert yourself or not. We believe that people worry excessively about the possibility of reprisals for expressing their opinions. As a result, they are inclined to use this excessive concern as an excuse or justification for not expressing their opinions. Remember, when you are trying hard not to express your opinions, you are still communicating something to your listener.

Some of the common counterproductive beliefs about expressing personal opinions and internal dialogues to dispute these beliefs are presented below. Discussion Module 3 contains additional suggestions for changing counterproductive beliefs and misconceptions.

Counterproductive beliefs about rights and responsibilities

I'm not smart enough, attractive enough, young enough, old enough, experienced enough, etc., to be entitled to express an opinion on that subject.

Is it true that I need to have special group membership in order to be entitled to express an opinion? Of course not. Everyone is entitled to his/her opinions. It is possible that special group membership could give me more experience or knowledge about the subject. Nevertheless, I am still entitled to my opinion, and I have the right to express it in an assertive manner.

Counterproductive beliefs about how I should behave or appear to others

If I voice my opinion and I am wrong, then how will I look?

I don't have to look any particular way to other people. What's so awful about being wrong? I can't always be right. No one is. If I am wrong, at least I'll know it, and I'll be able to rethink my opinion. Besides, most opinions are subjective and are not necessarily right or wrong. I'd rather be able to express my opinion than to sit there like a bump on a log and feel inhibited.

Counterproductive or erroneous beliefs about probable consequences

If the other person disagrees with my opinions, he/she won't like me, and then we'll get into an argument.

What evidence do I have that supports this belief? People can often disagree with each other on matters without disliking each other. No two people and no group of people can always agree on everything. If the other person doesn't like me for my views, that's up to him/her. have a right to express them as long as I do it assertively. Why does a disagreement have to result in an argument? All I plan to do is to assert my position and listen to what the other person has to say. If I feel that he/she is becoming aggressive, I can always break off communication by saying something such as, "Well, I understand your point of view, but I am still going to stand by my own views. Perhaps we could discuss it further at another time," or "I prefer that we do not discuss this any further since it seems that we have reached an impasse on this matter."

EXERCISE MODULE 11
SITUATIONS TO PRACTICE
EXPRESSING PERSONAL OPINIONS

Five situations are provided for you to practice expressing personal opinions. The comments of the other person are not always assertive. However, your task is to be assertive in your comments. In addition, model assertive responses for "you" are given for Situation 1. Remember to practice each situation as many times as you feel it is necessary. Also use the summary sheet on pages 77-78 when practicing the situations and evaluating your behavior. Finally, you are to design your own situations to practice and develop a list of real-life situations to use as homework assignments.

Situation 1

You and your spouse want to buy a new car. You need to express your personal opinions concerning cars in order to help make the decision on what to buy.

Spouse: I favor the larger cars.

You: _____

Spouse: Around town, a small car does have certain advantages.

You: _____

Spouse: How about a foreign car?

You: _____

Model Responses for Situation 1

Spouse: I favor the larger cars.
You: I think that a small car might be better.
Spouse: Around town, a small car does have certain advantages.
You: The small car would be more economical for us.
Spouse: How about a foreign car?
You: I don't know that much about foreign cars. Let me read up on them over the weekend and discuss it again then.

Situation 2

Your parents are discussing a new family who is planning to move in next door. You know these people and want to share your feelings about them with your family.

Parents: I hope these new people are good neighbors.
You: _____

Parents: I really will miss our old neighbors.
You: _____

Parents: I wonder what they're really like.
You: _____

Exercise Module 11

Situation 3

You are attending a seminar on health care practices. Presently, they are discussing the need for a clinic in your community to serve the elderly population. You have some strong feelings on this matter. You want to express them.

Seminar Member: The community is seriously considering such a clinic.
You: _____

Seminar Member: The financing of the clinic is one important aspect.
You: _____

Seminar Member: The clinic has been under consideration for some time.
You: _____

Situation 4

A friend is raving about a movie he/she just saw. You have seen it too, but thought it was unnecessarily violent and in bad taste. You want to express your point of view.

Friend: That movie was great. It seemed to really typify society today.
You: _____

Friend: I can't believe you didn't like it.
You: _____

Friend: You must have missed the whole point of it.
You: _____

Friend: Oh well, you can't please everybody.

Situation 5

You understand that the recreation center in your community is planning to evaluate the present procedures concerning summer programs and, if necessary, reorganize the existing procedures. Normally, the people in your community are not consulted but are expected to accept the changes. You decide you would like to give input this time. You have made an appointment with the director of the community center to discuss your ideas and ask to come to the next board meeting to talk with his staff.

Director: Come in, Ms./Mr. _____. What can I do for you?

You: _____

Director: Well, you know I'm very busy. Perhaps another time.

You: _____

Director: You really don't need to worry about that. We'll take care of your needs.

You: _____

Director: All right. When would be a convenient time?

Writing Your Own Practice Situations and Deciding on Homework Assignments

After you have practiced the above situations, you can write some personal situations that involve expressing personal opinions. You should develop situations that are likely to occur in your daily interactions and in which you feel you could use some practice. These situations also may be related to the homework assignments that you plan to try out in your environment. Remember, the main point of all the practice is to help you to express yourself in real-life interactions.

On the next two pages, space is provided to develop your own situations to practice. Space is also provided for you to jot down homework assignments.

Personal Situation—Expressing Personal Opinions

Describe Situation: _____
_____
_____

You: _____
_____

Other Person: _____
_____

You: _____
_____

Other Person: _____
_____

You: _____
_____

Personal Situation—Expressing Personal Opinions

Describe Situation: _____
_____
_____

You: _____
_____

Other Person: _____
_____

You: _____
_____

Other Person: _____
_____

You: _____
_____

Homework Assignment

List some possible situations in which you could practice expressing personal opinions when appropriate in your daily interactions. After you complete your list, star * a few you would like to begin with. Choose one for your first assignment in expressing personal opinions. You may find it helpful to rehearse your homework assignments before you try your new behavior in your daily interactions. Remember to start out with easy assignments first, and remember both to evaluate (criteria card in Discussion Module 4) and record (Tables 3 and 4) your behavior.

1.

2.

3.

4.

5.

6.

Chapter 4

Expressing Negative Feelings

Within the category expressing negative feelings, we have included the behaviors: expressing justified annoyance and displeasure and expressing justified anger. These behaviors involve expressing your unpleasant and negative feelings about a person to that person.

A general caution is in order with respect to the behaviors in this chapter. Obviously, it is less likely that people will respond in a friendly, positive manner to expressions of negative feelings than to expressions of positive feelings. Expressions of negative feelings, at times, can be met with anger, sarcasm, and even direct aggressive behavior. If negative feelings are expressed assertively, we believe that strong unfavorable reactions are not as likely to occur. Nevertheless, they are a possibility and should be borne in mind when (but not used as a rationalization against) deciding to assert negative feelings.

As we have mentioned in the introduction to the modules in Chapter Three, there are several ways to deal with unfavorable reactions to your assertions from other people. We will summarize these methods briefly, and we suggest that you review the material at the beginning of Chapter Three. First, inform significant others that you will be practicing assertive behavior and enlist their assistance. If unfavorable reactions occur, examine your behavior and the comments of the other person to determine whether your behavior was appropriate. Finally, restate your position and, if necessary, ignore the unfavorable reactions.

Another point concerns how you feel while you are expressing negative feelings. Expressing negative feelings may cause some discomfort for you. This is not unusual, since most of us do not enjoy giving others negative feedback even when it is necessary. Our point is that many people do not function at "0" Suds or even at a very low Suds level when they are expressing negative feelings. A mild level of discomfort may be unavoidable in such situations. However, the objective is to minimize that discomfort as much as possible and to endure it for the sake of the positive gains that you believe will result from asserting yourself in the situation.

In many ways the material in Discussion Modules 12 and 13 overlaps, since anger is often an extension or an intensification of feelings of annoyance and displeasure. As a result, you may find it helpful to read both of these modules.

Discussion Module **12**

Expressing Justified Annoyance and Displeasure

There are a number of situations in which you are justifiably annoyed or displeased by the behavior of another person: a close relative constantly teases you about your new boyfriend/girlfriend; your secretary continues to make the same mistake over and over after you have asked him/her repeatedly to correct it; someone violates your rights after you have indicated your position on the matter; your spouse comments on your weight problem when he/she knows how hard you are trying to stick to your diet; a subordinate continues to come to work late each morning; a friend or roommate borrows some jewelry without your permission. In all of these situations, you may feel justifiably annoyed or displeased, and if so, you have the right to express these feelings in an assertive manner. You also have the responsibility not to humiliate or demean the other person in the process. We trust that it is not your objective, when you express these feelings, to have the other person beg for your eternal forgiveness or throw himself/herself at your feet and plead for mercy.

What you are trying to accomplish is direct, nonaggressive communication of your feelings. Such an expression may or may not result in a change in the circumstances which originally caused your annoyance or displeasure. Sometimes it is too late to change the situation. However, by expressing your feelings you get these feelings off your mind so that you don't have to stew about them. In general, the purpose of expressing negative feelings is simply to relieve you of them as well as to make the other person aware of them so he/she doesn't repeat the same behavior again. We believe that, in most circumstances, it is better for you to express your justified annoyance and displeasure on the spot and hopefully resolve the matter than to carry these unpleasant feelings around with you.

As we mentioned earlier, expressing justified annoyance and displeasure assertively can be complicated by the fact that others may not respond favorably to such expressions. Such reactions probably can be minimized if a few general guidelines are observed when you formulate your verbal responses.

1. Keep your expression of annoyance and displeasure brief. Say exactly what you want to say initially. Once the other person has received the message, do not belabor or repeat it. That runs the risk of rubbing it in as well as the risk of escalating a mild annoyance into a full-scale war.
2. Don't make accusations or direct or indirect aggressive statements such as, "You are an inconsiderate so-and-so to have done that," or "Only people with very poor upbringing would do such a thing. By the way, where did you say you were raised?"
3. Incorporate "I" statements and "feeling talk" into the following three-part message:
   I (feel), when/because (behavior that caused the feeling). Next time, I would prefer that you (request for new behavior).

   You indicate in your message that you feel a certain way due to a specific behavior on the part of the other person. You also may wish to indicate to the other person how you would like him/her to behave in the future. The following statement is an example of how the general communication can be used.

   I am really *annoyed*, because you *didn't consider my opinion when you made that decision*. Next time, I would like you *to include me when you make a decision that affects both of us.*

   Such a message keeps the discussion on a more objective, less emotionally charged level.
4. If the other person wants to discuss or clarify the situation, then he/she has a right to be heard, but without belaboring the matter and without entering into an argument.
5. Use differential relaxation (Exercise Module 4) as a way of helping you cope with excessive anxiety that you feel before, during, or after the situation.

In the same manner that we do not encourage you to run around asking others to grant all sorts of unnecessary favors for the thrill of it (see Discussion Module 6), we also do not encourage you to spend your waking hours determining every little thing that annoys and displeases you in order to express annoyance simply for the principle of it. Being able to express justified annoyance and displeasure is a valuable skill; however, we advise you to use it appropriately.

Listed below are some common counterproductive beliefs about expressing justified annoyance and displeasure and internal dialogues for disputing them. You may want to refer to Discussion Module 3 for additional suggestions about changing counterproductive beliefs.

Counterproductive beliefs about rights and responsibilities

If I'm really his/her friend, I don't have any right to be annoyed. Real friends understand each other and don't get annoyed at each other.

What evidence do I have for this belief? Do I know anybody who has such a relationship? Of course not. The people who are really close are the ones who can get annoyed at each other from time to time and still remain friends. I guess in some ways being able to get annoyed at someone and then resolve it brings about a better understanding between the two people. Friendship involves a mutual give and take. If I am justifiably annoyed or displeased, I have the right to express it.

Counterproductive beliefs about how I should behave or appear to others

If I can't say something nice to someone, then I shouldn't say anything at all.

Does this belief help me to feel the way I want to feel or to avoid significant unpleasantness? It certainly seems rather difficult to do. When I'm annoyed at someone, it's hard for me to remain happy, cheerful, and pleasant. Usually I become less patient with them, and sometimes I even avoid them. I guess that I'm kidding myself if I think that by not telling them I'm annoyed that I'm concealing my feelings toward them. My feelings will leak out in other ways and may be subject to a great deal of misinterpretation. The other person may not understand what is happening with me and may think that the issue is a bigger deal than it really is. I can't expect that ignoring my annoyance will make it go away or will hide it from other people. It's better to express my annoyance. I hope that will clear the air.

Counterproductive or erroneous beliefs about probable consequences

If I express my displeasure, the outcome will be disastrous.

Is this belief true? I know that, when I assert myself, things don't always work out exactly the way I hope they will, but a disaster is unlikely. What am I afraid will happen? The other person will be angry at me? I might be wrong. The other person won't like me? Everyone can't like me. I'd rather express my annoyance and take the chance that someone won't like me or will be angry at me. I can cope with those possibilities better than walking around feeling annoyed for a long time. If I'm wrong, then I will apologize. I don't know of any magical formula that will allow me to determine beyond a shadow of a doubt whether my annoyance is appropriate in a particular situation. However, if I feel annoyed, then I have the right to express it in an assertive manner. If the other person thinks that my annoyance is misdirected or unjustified, he/she will tell me so, and then we can discuss it. If my intentions are sincere, the other person will probably understand how I feel and not hold it against me.

If I show my annoyance, the other person will use this annoyance against me, and try to get me more annoyed.

What evidence do I have for this belief? Most people are reasonable and will try to respect my feelings. If I meet someone who gets pleasure out of annoying me, I can either ignore the other person's childish attempts to provoke me or discontinue the relationship. At least, I have control over my behavior.

EXERCISE MODULE 12
SITUATIONS TO PRACTICE EXPRESSING
JUSTIFIED ANNOYANCE AND DISPLEASURE

Four situations are provided for you to practice expressing justified annoyance and displeasure. The comments of the other person are not always assertive. However, your task is to be assertive in your comments. In addition, model assertive responses for "you" are given for Situation 1. As you read the description for each situation, you will have to determine how you would feel in that situation. You may feel that you would be more than just annoyed or displeased. You may feel angry. If so, practice the particular situation along with Exercise Module 13 on expressing justified anger. It is difficult for us to know if you would feel annoyed or angered by a particular situation. Such a distinction is often based on previous interactions and the nature of the relationship.

Regardless of whether you are using the situations to practice expressing annoyance or anger (Discussion Module 13), remember to practice each situation as many times as you feel it is necessary. Also use the summary sheet on pages 77-78 when practicing the situations and evaluating your behavior. Finally, you are to design your own situations to practice and develop a list of real-life situations to use for homework assignments.

Situation 1

Your boss has set up three early morning meetings with you in the last two weeks. For these meetings, you had to get to work 45 minutes before you normally do. On all three occasions, he/she has cancelled the meeting via a phone call after you had arrived for the meeting. He/she has just asked you to come tomorrow morning for another early morning session.

Boss: Mr./Ms. _____, I need to see you tomorrow morning at 7:45.

You: _____

Boss: That couldn't be helped.

You: _____

Boss: It's very important that we get together.

You: _____

Boss: You're right. Next time, if I can't make it I'll call you no later than the evening before.

Model Responses for Situation 1

Boss:	Mr./Ms. _____, I need to see you tomorrow morning at 7:45.
You:	Mr./Ms. Smith, it's been annoying that I've come to three early morning appointments recently and you haven't been there.
Boss:	That couldn't be helped.
You:	7:45 A.M. is not very convenient for me, and it's quite annoying when you call after I get here.
Boss:	It's very important that we get together.
You:	I realize that, but I'd like to work out a better arrangement.
Boss:	You're right. Next time if I can't make it, I'll call you no later than the evening before.

Reminder: Notice how the request for new behavior—"I'd like to work out a better arrangement"—helps to resolve the situation.

Situation 2

You were assigned to work on a project with another colleague/classmate/worker in your office/class/organization about a month ago. You have been doing all the work by yourself. The project must be ready in five days, and you need his/her help if the project is to be completed by then. You decide to go and speak to this person.

You: _____

Coworker: You've been doing an excellent job.

You: _____

Coworker: I'm really very busy.

You: _____

Coworker: I know you can handle it.

You: _____

Coworker: You know, I guess I haven't been very helpful. Are you free after lunch today to get together?

Exercise Module 12

Situation 3

You and your spouse/friend/brother/sister/parent have one car that you share between the two of you. You have made plans to use the car tonight. Your spouse/friend/brother/sister/parent was made aware of your plans a week ago and agreed that you could have the car tonight. A half hour before you're ready to leave, your spouse/friend/brother/sister/parent decides he/she needs the car to go to a friend's house. He/she is getting into the car as you approach him/her.

You: _____

Other Person: I'm sorry, I need the car.

You: _____

Other Person: I don't want to be cooped up here all night again.

You: _____

Other Person: They are expecting me shortly.

You: _____

Other Person: Yes, but I need to get there.

You: _____

Other Person: You're right. I'm sure I can work something out.

Situation 4

Your spouse/boyfriend/girlfriend/friend was supposed to be home (or over) for dinner right after work. Instead, he/she arrives hours late and says that he/she was out with some friends from the office after work.

Spouse/Friend: Hi, I'm starved.

You: _____

Spouse/Friend: Dinner smells delicious.

You: _____

Spouse/Friend: Some of the people in my office stopped by Ron's house after work. He wanted to show us his new car.

You: _____

Spouse/Friend: You understand how these things are.

You: _____

Spouse/Friend: You're right. I should have been more considerate. I won't do that again.

Writing Your Own Practice Situations and Deciding on Homework Assignments

After you have practiced the above situations, you can write some personal situations that involve expressing justified annoyance or displeasure. You should develop situations that are likely to occur in your daily interactions and in which you feel you could use some practice. These situations also may be related to the homework assignments that you plan to try out in your environment. Remember, the main point of all the practice is to help you to express yourself in real-life interactions.

On the next two pages, space is provided to develop your own situations to practice. Space is also provided for you to jot down homework assignments.

Exercise Module 12

Personal Situation—Expressing Justified Annoyance and Displeasure

Describe Situation: _____
_____

You: _____
_____

Other Person: _____
_____

You: _____
_____

Other Person: _____
_____

You: _____
_____

Personal Situation—Expressing Justified Annoyance and Displeasure

Describe Situation: _____
_____

You: _____
_____

Other Person: _____
_____

You: _____
_____

Other Person: _____
_____

You: _____
_____

Homework Assignment

List some possible situations in which you could practice expressing justified annoyance and displeasure when appropriate in your daily interactions. After you complete your list, star * a few you would like to begin with. Choose one for your first assignment in expressing justified annoyance and displeasure. You may find it helpful to rehearse your homework assignments before you try your new behavior in your daily interactions. Remember to start out with easy assignments first, and remember both to evaluate (criteria card in Discussion Module 4) and record (Tables 3 and 4) your behavior.

1.

2.

3.

4.

5.

6.

Discussion Module **13**

Expressing Justified Anger

You have the right to express justified anger in an assertive manner to other people. You have the responsibility not to demean, humiliate, or abuse them in the process. We trust that your objective is not to force the other person to beg for forgiveness.

Many people have been taught that they should not feel anger or, at least, that they should not let other people know that they feel it, and above all, that they should not express it. It probably is impossible not to feel anger at some time, and we believe that it often is undesirable and even damaging to an individual or a relationship not to express justified anger when it is felt.

A major reason why people are taught not to express anger is because they are likely to become aggressive during such expressions. However, expressions of anger need not involve aggressive behavior. It is possible to raise one's voice, scowl, be very intense, and clearly indicate one's anger without threatening the other person, without insulting the other person, or being punitive or sarcastic. Granted this may not always be easy, it is an objective which you can work toward. By using "I" statements and the three-part message described in Discussion Module 12, you will reduce the likelihood that aggressive content will creep into your verbal behavior. Differential relaxation and changing counterproductive beliefs also will help reduce the aggressive content in both your verbal and nonverbal behavior.

We feel that it is important to be able to express justified anger in an assertive manner when it occurs. Anger is a volatile, potent emotional experience. It is difficult to bottle up and can lead to the development of psychological and psychosomatic complaints if it is frequently felt but seldom expressed. In addition, people usually communicate their angry feelings in one way or another. Many ways of expressing anger are not constructive. Some of these include: revenge, impatience with the person who caused the anger or with other people, avoidance of the person who caused the anger, blowing up at the person over a trivial or minor incident, and so on. We believe that you usually will feel better if you express your anger in an assertive manner when it occurs, and that such expressions ordinarily will clear the air between you and the other person(s). We refer you to Discussion Module 12 for tips on how to express your anger in a constructive manner. In summary, they are:

1. Be brief. Once you've made your point, don't belabor it.
2. Avoid making accusations.
3. Use "I" statements and the three-part communication.
4. Be willing to listen to the other person's point of view. End the conversation if it appears that it may result in an argument.

Some of the common misconceptions and counterproductive beliefs about expressing anger and internal dialogues for disputing those beliefs are discussed below. Discussion Modules 3 and 12 also contain helpful information.

Counterproductive beliefs about rights and responsibilities

There is something basically bad about people who make me angry. Bad people ought to pay for their behavior, and since no one else seems to be punishing them for it, I guess I will have to do so.

Why is this true? Who says that people who make me angry are necessarily bad? In most cases, they probably don't do it deliberately. Who says they should be punished, and even if they should who gave me the right to mete out justice? Besides, it doesn't help me to attain my goals without hurting others in the process.

Counterproductive beliefs about how I should behave or appear to others

If other people see me get angry, they will think that I am uptight, irrational, crazy, or ill-tempered.

This belief certainly doesn't help me to feel the way I want to feel. It gives me a choice between two unpleasant feelings; remaining angry if I don't express my feelings, or feeling embarrassed if I express my feelings and someone witnesses the spectacle. I cannot control what others think. If they look down on me for expressing my anger, that's their right. At least, I won't have to carry that anger with me, and they may respect me for being able to express my anger without becoming aggressive.

Counterproductive or erroneous beliefs about probable consequences

If I express my anger, the other person will fall apart.

Is this true, and does it help me to avoid significant unpleasantness without denying my rights? First, most people do not fall apart when others are angry at them. In some cases, they get upset for a short period of time, but that's about all. If I am dealing with a person who is very sensitive to anger or criticism, I can choose my words accordingly if necessary. However, I shouldn't use that as an excuse not to express how I feel, particularly if I'm going to feel worse as a result. Most people can cope with anger, and if I express it assertively then it's less of a problem for them.

EXERCISE MODULE 13
SITUATIONS TO PRACTICE
EXPRESSING JUSTIFIED ANGER

Four situations are provided for you to practice expressing justified anger. The comments of the other person are not always assertive. However, your task is to be assertive in your comments. In addition, model assertive responses for "you" are given for Situation 1. As you read the descriptions for each situation, you will have to determine how you would feel in that situation. You may feel that you would not be angry, but rather annoyed or displeased with the other person. If so, practice the particular situation as if it were a situation in Exercise Module 12 on expressing justified annoyance or displeasure. It is difficult for us to know if you would feel annoyed or angered by a particular situation. Such a distinction is based on previous interactions and the nature of the relationship.

Regardless of whether you are using the situations to practice expressing anger or annoyance (Discussion Module 12), remember to practice each situation as many times as you feel it is necessary. Also use the summary sheet on pages 77-78 when practicing the situations and evaluating your behavior. Finally, you are to design your own situations to practice and develop a list of real-life situations to use for homework assignments.

Situation 1

You have a car pool with two other persons. Supposedly you all have to get to work by 9:00 A.M. One of the members of your car pool has not been very dependable. He/she has only driven about once every two weeks, has failed to call on four occasions when he/she wasn't going to work with you in the morning, and has caused you to be late on a number of mornings. Yesterday was the final straw. He/she was supposed to drive and never showed up. This morning when you pick this person up, you plan to express your anger about yesterday.

Rider: Good morning.

You: _____

Rider: I must have mentioned that I was thinking about taking the day off.

You: _____

Rider: Well, if I didn't show up by 8:40 you should have figured I wasn't coming.

You: _____

Rider: I guess I've really inconvenienced you, but you see I don't have to be at work every day nor be in by 9:00. I think it would be better if I went by myself. Sorry about yesterday.

Model Responses for Situation 1

Rider:	Good morning.
You:	Dick/Debbie, I am quite angry about yesterday. You were supposed to pick me up and you never came. I would like you to call me with plenty of time to spare if you're not going to pick me up.
Rider:	I must have mentioned that I was thinking about taking the day off.
You:	When you left the day before, you said "I'll pick you up tomorrow."
Rider:	Well, if I didn't show up by 8:40 you should have figured I wasn't coming.
You:	Dick/Debbie, what you just said makes me even angrier. You said you were going to pick me up and unless I heard differently or an emergency or an accident occurred, I *expected* to be picked up. Next time, please call.
Rider:	I guess I've really inconvenienced you, but you see I don't have to be at work every day nor be in by 9:00. I think it would be better if I went by myself. Sorry about yesterday.
Reminder:	Notice how the use of the three part communication described in Discussion Module 12 helps in expressing your anger and in resolving the matter.

Situation 2

One of your neighbors has developed the habit of going into your tool shed/house/garage and taking anything he/she wants. You have told your neighbor at least twice already that you want him/her to ask to borrow your things before taking them. You just noticed that one of your paint brushes is missing. You know your neighbor has planned to paint his/her kitchen today. You decide to go over to your neighbor's house and tell him/her that you are angry because you have requested that he/she asks first.

You: _____

Neighbor: It's just a paint brush.

You: _____

Neighbor: I don't see what the problem is.

You: _____

Neighbor: I will check with you first in the future.

You: _____

Neighbor: I really need to finish my painting now. How about coming over in about 3 hours to see how it looks? See you then.

Exercise Module 13

Situation 3

Your "friend" has been spreading rumors about you. He/she is telling others that you outstay your welcome when you're invited to other homes. You know that this is not so because you have checked with others just to be sure. You are quite angry with your friend for spreading this rumor. You want to express your anger toward him/her. However, you do not want to break off this relationship if at all possible.

You: _____

Friend: I haven't said anything.
You: _____

Friend: Look, I really didn't say anything.
You: _____

Friend: You sure are touchy today. Who are you angry at? Your mom?
You: _____

Friend: Well, if that's how you feel, I won't say anything about you.
You: _____

Friend: See you later, perhaps.

Situation 4

Your parents are always telling you how to run your life. You have requested that they do not continue to do this. Yesterday your parents really outdid themselves. They called your spouse's/boyfriend's/girlfriend's parents to try and discourage you and your spouse/boyfriend/girlfriend from going to the beach over a holiday weekend. You are quite angry, since you feel your parents are overstepping their limits.

You: _____

Parents: You never listen to me.

You: _____

Parents: I know what is best for you.

You: _____

Parents: I feel you act too impulsively. I'm not hurting anyone.

You: _____

Parents: I'm sorry you feel this way, but I really am worried about you. However, I guess I may be overdoing it.

Writing Your Own Practice Situations and Deciding on Homework Assignments

After you have practiced the above situations, you can write some personal situations that involve expressing justified anger. You should develop situations that are likely to occur in your daily interactions and in which you feel you could use some practice. These situations also may be related to the homework assignments that you plan to try out in your environment. Remember, the main point of all the practice is to help you to express yourself in real-life interactions.

On the next two pages, space is provided to develop your own situations to practice. Space is also provided for you to jot down homework assignments.

Exercise Module 13

Personal Situation—Expressing Justified Anger

Describe Situation: _____
_____
_____

You: _____
_____

Other Person: _____
_____

You: _____
_____

Other Person: _____
_____

You: _____
_____

Personal Situation—Expressing Justified Anger

Describe Situation: _____
_____
_____

You: _____
_____

Other Person: _____
_____

You: _____
_____

Other Person: _____
_____

You: _____
_____

chapter 4: Expressing Negative Feelings

Homework Assignment

List some possible situations in which you could practice expressing justified anger when appropriate in your daily interactions. After you complete your list, star * a few you would like to begin with. Choose one for your first assignment in expressing justified anger. You may find it helpful to rehearse your homework assignments before you try your new behavior in your daily interactions. Remember to start out with easy assignments first, and remember both to evaluate (criteria card in Discussion Module 4) and record (Tables 3 and 4) your behavior.

1.

2.

3.

4.

5.

6.

Chapter 5

Assertion in Special Situations and with Special People

The situations in this chapter share the fact that the roles of the persons involved in the interactions appear to possess special obligations and rules of conduct which have implications for assertive behavior. The general guidelines and rights of assertive behavior are the same, but an understanding of the special complexities of these situations will help you to function more effectively in them.

Discussion Module **14**

Assertion with Parents and Other Family Members

People often report having difficulty asserting themselves with parents or parents-in-law well beyond their adolescent years, the period in which such issues typically are resolved. There probably are at least two major issues from the offspring's perspective that are involved in assertion with parents. The first is dependency versus independency. The process of growing up involves a gradual shift from being dependent and unequal in rights and privileges in a relationship to being independent and totally equal in rights and privileges in our society. As a baby, you obviously are totally dependent on your parents and have few rights other than those for food, shelter, and comfort. As you grow up, you develop skills and abilities, and you assume and are granted increasing authority to make your own decisions as well as more rights and privileges. Ideally, the transition is a smooth one, so that by the time you reach adulthood you are independent and equal to your parents in rights and privileges.

Another issue is that of respect and obligation. We learn to respect our parents when we grow up. We respect them as children because they are older, wiser, and, we believe, more capable, and because they provide for us. We also are obligated to obey them. When we become adults, the nature of respect and obligation change. Respect and obligation now involve a relationship between two equal parties, in much the same manner as for any other adults.

For parents, a major change in the relationship is also in order as children become adults. This change involves the gradual relinquishing of control in the relationship. Just as it may be difficult for many people as they become adults to assume independence and leave behind the old securities of having someone take care of them and make decisions for them, it also can be difficult for parents to relinquish control and leave behind the security of having someone be dependent on them. For parents, the fact that their children are becoming adults signals the beginning of a new stage of life. It means growing older, having to develop new relationships to replace those with the children, and so on. Such a readjustment can be a difficult one as well as one which is resisted by trying to keep the children dependent through inducing guilt or by imposing obligations.

In most instances, problems of assertion with parents revolve around the legitimate right of being able to make your own decisions and live your own life. One concern that many people have is to be able to communicate this right and, at the same time, to show concern for their parents' feelings. One way to do this is through the use of an empathic assertion.*

An empathic assertion involves responding with an acknowledgment or a statement of appreciation for the other person's concern while maintaining your position at the same time; for example, "Mother/Father, I appreciate that you are concerned about me and that you want the best for me. However, I feel that it is in my own best interest to do something else." We advise you to use an empathic assertion only if you believe that it is appropriate. If you feel that your parents' concerns are attempts to induce guilt or a false sense of obligation, then you can indicate that to them and request that they not make such comments in the future.

Assertion with parents can be particularly difficult at the time that a person legally becomes an adult and shortly thereafter. At this time, people can be either somewhat unsure about their rights for independent decision-making or somewhat afraid to assume these rights. One way to cope with this new status is to ask yourself how you would feel and act if you were fifty years old. How about at forty-five? forty? thirty-five? Usually you will find little uncertainty as you assume the position of being older. You know what you would do. As you bring the age closer to your own, you realize that your concern is reluctance to exercise your rights even though you are an adult. At some point you will have to do so. Why not start now?

Discussed below are some counterproductive beliefs concerning assertion with parents and internal dialogues for disputing them. Dicussion Module 3 contains some additional suggestions that may be helpful.

Counterproductive beliefs about rights and responsibilities

They must have spent a small fortune raising me in addition to the time and emotional commitment that was involved. After all they have done for me, I don't have the right to go against their wishes in my decisions.

Why is this so? When they decided to have me, they knew that it would be expensive. Most people know about the financial obligation and emotional commitment that is involved in raising children. People freely choose to take on that obligation when they become parents. I don't see how they can make me indebted for a financial obligation they willingly assumed. It's not fair to me. Besides, I have the right to make my own decisions.

I have the responsibility to help my parents solve my brother's/sister's (emotional, financial, marital, etc.) problems. After all, they are my parents, and he/she is my brother/sister.

Is this true? How much obligation do I really have? I have my own life to live and my own problems. I can only do so much, and I only want to do so much. We are all adults. Adults are supposed to be able to solve their own problems. I will devote only as much time and help as I want, and only in the way that I choose.

---

*P. Jakubowski-Spector, *An Introduction to Assertive Training Procedures for Women.* Washington, D.C.: American Personnel and Guidance Association, 1973.

Counterproductive beliefs about how I should behave or appear to others

If they want us to go to dinner every Friday, we should go to dinner with them. Look, they still are providing some financial support. If they want us to take them shopping, etc., they are providing financial support.

Is this true? Is this money a loan, a gift, a job or what? Perhaps I need to have a better understanding of what we agreed to when we accepted this money. We still maintain the right to make our own decisions and live our own lives—or do we?

Counterproductive or erroneous beliefs about probable consequences

If I don't make the decisions they want me to, they will be upset with me.

Although this often is true, it doesn't help me to avoid significant unpleasantness without denying my rights. We are all adults. Some adults are not going to like the decisions made by other adults. It's regrettable if they are not pleased with me, but I have to decide how I want to live. I have to govern my decisions by my wishes not by those of someone else.

If I don't go along with my parents, they will "fall apart." After all, they are getting old, and one's elders deserve special consideration.

Does this belief help me to feel the way I want to feel? It does not. By treating my parents with kid gloves, I become impatient and annoyed. I really don't enjoy them as much anymore. In addition, I treat them as if they are helpless rather than mature adults. If anyone treated me in this fashion, I would be irritated. I think I will begin treating them with the same respect and consideration that I treat my friends. Since my friends do not fall apart, I doubt that my parents will.

Discussion Module 14

EXERCISE MODULE 14
SITUATIONS TO PRACTICE ASSERTION
WITH PARENTS AND OTHER FAMILY MEMBERS

Four situations are provided in this module for you to practice expressing yourself with your parents and other family members. In addition to these situations, situations dealing with parents and family members are provided in Exercise Module 7, Situation 3; Exercise Module 9, Situation 4; Exercise Module 11, Situation 2; and Exercise Module 13, Situation 4.

Each situation in this exercise module is labeled with the type of behavior called for, such as expressing legitimate rights, giving a compliment, expressing annoyance. If you have difficulty with a situation, read the discussion module dealing with the particular behavior under consideration.

In each situation provided for you to practice, the comments of the parent or other family member are not always assertive. However, your task is to be assertive in your comments. In addition, model assertive responses for "you" are given for Situation 1. Remember to practice each situation as many times as you feel it is necessary. Also use the summary sheet on pages 77-78 when practicing the situations and evaluating your behavior. Finally, you are to design your own situations to practice and develop a list of real-life situations to use as homework assignments.

Situation 1–Expressing Annoyance and Standing Up for Your Rights

Your parents/parents-in-law keep telling you how you are supposed to raise your children. You've told them on numerous occasions not to discipline your children in your home when you are present. Your family, including your parents/parents-in-law has just finished dinner. Your parents/parents-in-law have scolded your children three times this evening. You want to express your annoyance and ask them to stop. You talk to them after the children have gone to bed.

You: _____

Parents/In-Laws: They'll never learn the correct way.

You: _____

Parents/In-Laws: You could use my experience. I did raise three children.

You: _____

Parents/In-Laws: If that's how you feel about it—but remember, I tried to help you.

176 chapter 5: Assertion in Special Situations and with Special People

Model Responses for Situation 1

You: I'm really annoyed about this evening, because I don't want you scolding the kids. As I've mentioned before, I'd appreciate it if you did not interfere.

Parents/In-Laws: They'll never learn the correct way.

You: I appreciate your concern, but I want to bring them up the way I feel is appropriate. They are my kids.

Parents/In-Laws: You could use my experience. I did raise three children.

You: And now it's my turn to raise my children, so I would like you to keep your opinions to yourself about how I raise my children, especially when the children are around.

Parents/In-Laws: If that's how you feel about it—but remember, I tried to help you.

Reminder: Notice the use of the empathic assertion "I appreciate your concern, but . . ."

Situation 2–Giving a Compliment or Expressing Liking and Affection

Your brother/sister/parent has been very helpful lately. You had a lot of work to do and he/she has voluntarily given up some of his/her time. If you hadn't received this help, you're not sure you could have met all your deadlines. You want to express your appreciation to your brother/sister/parent.

You: _____

Relative: You would have done the same for me.

You: _____

Relative: I'm glad I could help you.

You: _____

Relative: It makes me feel good to hear you say those things about me.

Reminder: Be sure to say what you really want to. If you want to thank your relative, do that. If you want to tell him/her how much you like him/her for his/her help, say that.

Exercise Module 14

Situation 3—Asking a Favor

You need to ask your parents or another close relative if you can borrow $25 until your next paycheck. You need to make a payment and can't wait until next week when you get paid. You do not want to explain what you need the money for. You will pay them back in a week from today.

You: _____

Parents/Relative: Are you in some trouble?
You: _____

Parents/Relatives Can't you manage your money better?
You: _____

Parents/Relative: Here, but I want it back next week.
You: _____

Reminder: You need not make excuses for asking for this money. Be sure you are not begging or pleading. You have a right to ask. Your parents or relatives also have a right to say yes or no. In the above example, a definitive no was never given.

Situation 4 – Refusing a Request

Your parent/relative asks you to babysit for them tonight. Although you don't mind babysitting for them, you already have plans for tonight and do not want to babysit.

Parent/Relative: Jack/Jane, I need you to babysit tonight.

You: _____

Parent/Relative: Oh, you can change your plans. I'll even bake your favorite cake for you.

You: _____

Parent/Relative: I was really counting on you for tonight. I don't know what I'll do.

You: _____

Reminder: You need not feel obligated or guilty in this situation. You can't be expected to comply with every request.

Writing Your Own Practice Situations and Deciding on Homework Assignments

After you have practiced the above situations, you can write some personal situations that involve asserting yourself with parents or relatives. You should develop situations which are likely to occur in your daily interactions and in which you feel you could use some practice. These situations also may be related to the homework assignments that you plan to try out in your environment. Remember, the main point of all the practice is to help you to express yourself in real-life interactions.

On the next two pages, space is provided to develop your own situations to practice. Space is also provided for you to jot down homework assignments.

Exercise Module 14

Personal Situation—Asserting Yourself with Parents or Other Family Members

Describe Situation: _____
_____
_____

You: _____
_____

Parent/Relative: _____
_____

You: _____
_____

Parent/Relative: _____
_____

You: _____
_____

Personal Situation—Asserting Yourself with Parents or Other Family Members

Describe Situation: _____
_____
_____

You: _____
_____

Parent/Relative: _____
_____

You: _____
_____

Parent/Relative: _____
_____

You: _____
_____

Homework Assignment

List some possible situations in which you could practice asserting yourself with parents and other family members in your daily interactions. After you complete your list, star * a few you would like to begin with. Choose one for your first assignment in asserting yourself with parents and other family members. You may find it helpful to rehearse your homework assignments before you try your new behavior in your daily interactions. Remember to start out with easy assignments first, and remember both to evaluate (criteria card in Discussion Module 4) and record (Tables 3 and 4) your behavior.

1.

2.

3.

4.

5.

6.

Discussion Module **15**

Assertion with Authority Figures

Bosses, teachers and professors, administrators, doctors, lawyers, and public officials are examples of authority figures that people sometimes have difficulty interacting with in an assertive manner. All of these people occupy positions which give them some type of power over us. The types of power that they possess vary but can include: the power to control salary and budgets, the power to deny or retard progress toward future goals, the power to control privileges and duties, the power to control access to needed information, the power to control needed resources, and the possession of superior knowledge.

Assertion with authority figures may be difficult for some people for at least two reasons. Since the authority possesses certain types of power, we often seem to concede special human rights to him/her. In comparison, we seem to deny ourselves certain human rights. In many ways it appears to be almost a matter of increasing the rights of the authority while diminishing our own rights. In reality, there is no reason for this. The authority may possess greater power, but not greater rights.

A second point is that people often believe that if they behave in ways that are unpopular with the authority, the authority will use (misuse) his/her power against them. This is a distinct possibility and should be taken into account; however, it is probably the fear or the expectation of negative consequences rather than the likely occurrence of these consequences that prevents most people from asserting themselves with authorities. We believe that authority figures tend to respond favorably to assertive requests, assertive disagreements, and assertive interactions when they are appropriate (in time, place, and so on). People often make a big deal out of interactions with authorities by worrying that disastrous, but highly improbable, consequences are sure to be forthcoming. There usually are checks and balances in any system that thwart the misuse of power before it occurs or that can correct a grievance after it has occurred. An unfair grade can be appealed to a higher authority, employment grievances can be brought to the attention of arbitrators, and so on.

As we stated in other modules, we caution you against asserting yourself routinely and unnecessarily simply to prove that you can do so. For example, there is nothing to be gained—except for a reputation as a nuisance or troublemaker—by asserting yourself with your boss about every little detail of your job or of his/her behavior that doesn't meet completely with your approval. The effect of such assertions is to make it less likely that he/she will pay attention to you when you have an important concern to voice.

Some of the common counterproductive beliefs concerning assertion with authority figures that we have encountered and internal dialogues for disputing them are listed below. See Discussion Module 3 for other suggestions about changing counterproductive beliefs and misconceptions.

Counterproductive beliefs about rights and responsibilities

Since Professor Jamison is such a well-known expert in that area, someone like me can't just question his/her position on that issue.

Why is this so? What I'm telling myself is that I'm not worthy enough, that I don't have the right to say I don't understand, or that I can't say that his/her position is not defensible to me. Maybe I'm even saying that I don't want to appear ignorant. At any rate, I am denying my right to raise questions and to ask for clarification. I have the right to ask questions or to disagree with another person. If I deny this right, in essence, I am saying that this other person is entitled to certain rights and privileges because of his/her position and I am not.

Counterproductive beliefs about how I should behave or appear to others

If my boss frequently asks me to work late or do special favors, I should do it. (Otherwise, he/she will consider me to be uncooperative.)

Does this help me to feel the way I want to feel? I don't mind doing extra tasks or working late sometimes, epsecially if I'm getting paid for it. But after a while it becomes an imposition, and I resent having to do it. I have the right to say no if this is how I feel about it. The fact that he/she is my boss does not change my rights or how I should behave. If I don't want to work late, I don't have to. I need not worry about how it looks to others. I can make my own decisions.

Counterproductive or erroneous beliefs about probable consequences

If I state my opinion, he/she will deny my raise, deprive me of my legitimate privileges, turn down my legitimate request, etc., as a way of penalizing me for saying what I think.

Is this true? Well, it certainly is possible. I know people who seek revenge when others say things that they don't like. However, it doesn't occur that frequently. It sure doesn't make me feel the way I want to feel if I have something to say, but live in fear of reprisals if I say it and it proves to be unpopular. I have to decide whether I will feel better if I say it, taking my chances about the consequences, or feel better if I stifle my feelings. Besides, in the unlikely event that he/she uses his/her power against me because of what I say, I usually can appeal my dilemma to a higher authority.

EXERCISE MODULE 15
SITUATIONS TO PRACTICE ASSERTION
WITH AUTHORITY FIGURES

Four situations are provided in this module for you to practice expressing yourself with authority figures. In addition to these situations, situations dealing with authority figures are provided in Exercise Module 6, Situation 3; Exercise Module 9, Situation 2; Exercise Module 11, Situation 5; and Exercise Module 12, Situation 1.

Each situation in this exercise module is labeled with the type of behavior called for, such as expressing legitimate rights, giving a compliment, refusing a request. If you have difficulty with a situation, read the discussion module dealing with the particular behavior under consideration.

In each situation provided for you to practice, the comments of the authority figures are not always assertive. However, your task is to be assertive in your comments. In addition, model assertive responses for "you" are given for Situation 1. Remember to practice each situation as many times as you feel it is necessary. Also use the summary sheet on pages 77-78 when practicing the situations and evaluating your behavior. Finally, you are to design your own situations to practice and develop a list of real-life situations to use as homework assignments.

Situation 1–Standing Up for Your Rights

Your physician has just given you a prescription to get filled for the stomach discomfort you've been having. You want to know what the prescription is and what the potential side effects might be. Your doctor is generally quite vague on these issues.

You: _____

Physician: It's name is not important. Just take two teaspoons after each meal and give me a call in five days or so.

You: _____

Physician: Don't worry, just call me if you have any more difficulties.

You: _____

Physician: It's called _____. It contains an antibiotic for the bacteria and an ingredient to coat your stomach. You shouldn't experience any problems. However, if your temperature goes up or if your stomach doesn't feel better by tomorrow afternoon, call me.

You: _____

Model Responses for Situation 1

You: Dr. Carps, what is this medicine called that you have recommended for me?

Physician: It's name is not important. Just take two teaspoons after each meal and give me a call in five days or so.

You: Dr. Carps, I'd like to know what this medicine is called and what it does.

Physician: Don't worry, just call me if you have any more difficulties.

You: Dr. Carps, I'm not planning to take any medicine if I don't know what it is, what it does, and what possible side effects it may cause. I feel I have a right to this information.

Physician: It's called _____. It contains an antibiotic for the bacteria and an ingredient to coat your stomach. You shouldn't experience any problems. However, if your temperature goes up or if your stomach doesn't feel better by tomorrow afternoon, call me.

You: Thank you for the information, Dr. Carps. I'll call you if I have any problems.

Reminder: You have the right to request and receive information from your physician. Be direct in your request. It is your body, and you should know what is being prescribed for you.

Situation 2 – Giving a Compliment

You are attending a workshop/class. The professor has just completed his/her presentation. It was one of the best presentations you have heard. You want to tell the professor how you feel.

You: _____

Professor: I'm glad you feel that way.

You: _____

Professor: Thank you for stopping to tell me. How about joining me for lunch?

Exercise Module 15

Situation 3 – Refusing a Request

Your boss has made a number of extra demands on you lately. When you have the time, you don't mind helping him out. However, this week, he/she has asked for too many favors. Yesterday, he/she had you drop off a package on your way home, and today he/she wants you to pick up a check on your way home. These demands are interfering with your plans at home. You need to tell your boss you can't help him/her today.

Boss: Bob/Betty, I need a check to be picked up at 6:00 tonight.
You: _____

Boss: It's important that we have that check tomorrow.
You: _____

Boss: I don't know who else could do it.
You: _____

Boss: All right, I'll pick it up at 7 P.M. on my way to my card game.

Situation 4 – Making a Request

You would like to attend a play that your child is in at school. You need to leave work early to see it. You want to ask your boss for some time off this afternoon.

Boss: Come in.
You: _____

Boss: We're quite busy today.
You: _____

Boss: Okay, but just this time.

Writing Your Own Practice Situations and Deciding on Homework Assignments

After you have practiced the above situations, you can write some personal situations that involve asserting yourself with authority figures. You should develop situations that are likely to occur in your daily interactions and in which you feel you could use some practice. These situations also may be related to the homework assignments that you plan to try out in your environment. Remember, the main point of all the practice is to help you to express yourself in real-life interactions.

On the next two pages, space is provided to develop your own situations to practice. Space is also provided for you to jot down homework assignments.

Personal Situation—Assertion with Authority Figures

Describe Situation: _____
_____
_____

You: _____
_____

Other Person: _____
_____

You: _____
_____

Other Person: _____
_____

You: _____
_____

Personal Situation—Assertion with Authority Figures

Describe Situation: _____
_____
_____

You: _____
_____

Other Person: _____
_____

You: _____
_____

Other Person: _____
_____

You. _____
_____

Homework Assignment

List some possible situations in which you could practice asserting yourself with authority figures in your daily interactions. After you complete your list, star * a few you would like to begin with. Choose one for your first assignment in asserting yourself with authority figures. You may find it helpful to rehearse your homework assignments before you try your new behavior in your daily interactions. Remember to start out with easy assignments first, and remember both to evaluate (criteria card in Discussion Module 4) and record (Tables 3 and 4) your behavior.

1.

2.

3.

4.

5.

6.

Discussion Module **16**

Assertion in Couples

The emotional bonds that exist in couples or other close personal relationships have special implications for assertive behavior and assertion training. The first implication concerns the nature of the relationship between the members of the couple and the effect that assertion training may have on that relationship.

Members of a couple establish ways of relating to each other which become fairly predictable to each other after a short time. If one member of the couple seeks to become more assertive, the manner of relating in the couple may be altered in some ways. If the second member of the couple has been profiting from the first member's nonassertive behavior in the relationship, the second member may not be happy about the change, at least initially. The second member either will have to try to adjust or to thwart further assertive behavior. This can be particularly true with married couples.

For example, suppose that both members of the couple work and have very busy schedules. One member expects that when he/she has free time, the other member should be available and enthusiastic about dropping whatever he/she is doing in order for them to spend time together. The second member complies with this expectation even though he/she is often tired and resents having to be the Johnny-on-the-spot. If the second member asserts himself/herself and states that he/she intends to be available only if he/she has been given enough time to rearrange the schedule, the first member may not react favorably to the assertion. If adjustments do not occur, then it is conceivable that the relationship might end.

On the other hand, if a lack of assertive behavior has strained the relationship, then the second party will welcome assertive behavior even though it may involve a readjustment in the relationship. For instance, suppose

chapter 5: Assertion in Special Situations and with Special People that one member of a couple consistently has to make all the major decisions for the couple. The second member repeatedly indicated that anything is all right with him/her because he/she is worried about recommending a decision that might be unpopular. However, the decision-maker feels uncomfortable about having to assume responsibility for the two of them. Under these circumstances, the first member of the couple would welcome more frequent expressions of personal opinions from the second member.

The point is that learning to behave assertively can change the typical manner in which the members of a couple relate to each other, and it is important for both parties to be aware of this fact. Assertive behavior assumes that the members of the couple have equal rights in the relationship. If equality is desirable but does not presently exist, then it might be helpful for both members of the couple to attempt to develop their assertive skills together as a way of understanding more clearly how they relate to each other. In those instances in which only one member of a couple is involved in assertion training, it is important for that person to prepare the other member to expect new behaviors and possible changes in the relationship. Preparing the other member can be accomplished by explaining the importance of assertive behavior and by providing him/her with appropriate reading materials. This preparation can often result in your receiving much needed support and encouragement for your new behavior while minimizing the possibility of stress in the relationship.

A second implication is that with the added closeness and attachment that is involved in a couple relationship certain assumptions about rights, responsibilities, and ways of behaving often are made. Many of these assumptions go beyond those which exist in other relationships and often are either erroneous or counterproductive. We discuss some of these assumptions and ways of disputing them next.

Counterproductive beliefs about rights and responsibilities

If I really love him/her, I don't have the right to inconvenience him/her. I'll ask someone else for help.

Why is this true? What I'm saying is if I love someone, then I put them on a pedestal and give them certain privileges that I don't give others. I guess that makes some sense, but am I carrying it too far? I have the right to make requests. I'm being overly sensitive about inconveniencing the ones I love. Perhaps I weaken the relationship by not making legitimate requests now and then.

If he/she really loves me, then he/she should cater to all my wishes, should wait on me hand and foot, and should spend almost all of his/her free time with me.

Does this belief help me to achieve my goals without infringing on the rights of others? It sounds as though I'm expecting the other person to be an adoring servant in this relationship rather than an equal partner with needs and preferences of his/her own. Having a close relationship with this person does not give me the right to be so possessive and demanding.

Counterproductive beliefs about how I should behave or appear to others

If I really love him/her, I should know how he/she would feel on that matter without having to ask. Then I should behave accordingly.

What evidence do I have for this belief? What I'm saying is that, if I am really close to someone, I should have ESP and be able to read his/her mind. That doesn't follow. When you know someone well, you sometimes can anticipate how they feel about things. But what I'm saying is that if I love a person, I am obligated to know his/her every thought. I'm jumping to the conclusion that if I don't know his/her thoughts, then I don't really love him/her or there is something wrong with the relationship. I'm really making impossible demands of myself. I will know how he/she feels only if I ask.

If we've been together this long, he/she should know now I feel about him/her. I shouldn't have to show or tell him/her how I feel.
What evidence do I have for this belief? Why do I think that once I tell someone how I feel that he/she will realize that I will continue to feel that way? People's feelings can change over time. If I still feel the same way, I have to tell the other person now and then. Otherwise, he/she won't have any way to know how I feel.

Counterproductive or erroneous beliefs about probable consequences

If I like/love him/her and I criticize some aspect of his/her behavior, he/she will be terribly upset and fall apart.
What evidence do I have for this belief? What I'm saying is that people who like/love each other are overly sensitive to justified criticism from each other. At times this may be true. However, it also may be true that they are more able to accept and use criticism, since they know that the other person genuinely cares and would not knowingly hurt them. Further, if I don't express my criticism, it's not going to help me feel the way I want to feel, and it won't help the relationship. I know that I will be annoyed if I don't say something, and that annoyance will be revealed in other ways. It's better to express my feelings now and clear the air than let them build up.

After we've been going together for so long, I can't just tell him/her that I don't love him/her anymore. That would be too devastating. I'll just break the news gently. I'll ease myself out of the relationship. I'll let him/her down easily. I won't call as often, or I'll have a friend tell him/her it's over.
Does this belief help me to achieve my goals and to do so without hurting others? No matter how I break off the relationship, it's going to be unpleasant. But is this the best way to do it? If I were in his/her position, what would make me feel least upset? Having it end once and for all? Or having it string out over several months? I guess I'd rather know that it was over and part company once and for all than to have the agony stretch out over a long time. It would be easier for both of us, as well as more considerate, if I told him/her directly how I feel.

If I don't go along with his/her wishes, he/she will withdraw love, support, help, companionship, etc., from me, and I will be alone.
Does this belief help me to avoid significant unpleasantness without simultaneously denying my rights? Do I know that this will really happen, or am I upsetting myself unnecessarily. Furthermore, how do I feel about myself when I accede to his/her wishes against my better judgment? I know I don't feel very good about myself. In fact, I often feel cut off from him/her, left out, alone. I'm allowing myself to be the victim of emotional blackmail. I'm also making it more likely that he/she will threaten to withdraw love, etc., in the future if I don't agree to his/her wishes. I'll probably be better off if I express my rights and take the consequences than if I deny my feelings. He/she may even respect me more for expressing my wishes.

EXERCISE MODULE 16
SITUATIONS TO PRACTICE
ASSERTION IN COUPLES

Four situations are provided for you to practice asserting yourself with your partner. In addition to these situations, situations for assertion in couples are provided in Exercise Module 5, Situation 2; Exercise Module 11, Situation 1; and Exercise Module 12, Situations 3 and 4.

Each situation in this exercise module is labeled with the type of behavior called for, such as standing up for your rights, expressing personal opinions, and so on. If you have difficulty with a situation, read the discussion module dealing with the particular behavior under consideration.

In each situation provided for you to practice, the comments of the other person are not always assertive. However, your task is to be assertive in your comments. In addition, model assertive responses for "you" are given for Situation 1. Remember to practice each situation as many times as you feel it is necessary. Also use the summary sheet on pages 77-78 when practicing the situations and evaluating your behavior. Finally, you are to design your own situations to practice and develop a list of real-life situations to use as homework assignments.

Situation 1–Standing Up for Your Rights

You feel that your spouse/boyfriend/girlfriend has been making too many demands on your time. You are expected to drop whatever you are doing when he/she wants your companionship or when he/she wants you to do something. You feel as if you are being taken for granted. You feel it is time to tell your spouse/boyfriend/girlfriend how you feel and work out a better arrangement, if possible.

You: _____

Spouse/Boy/Girl: I don't understand.

You: _____

Spouse/Boy/Girl: We must have a misunderstanding.

You: _____

Spouse/Boy/Girl: I really appreciate you, so I'm not sure I really understand.

You: _____

Spouse/Boy/Girl: Okay, we'll have to work out a better arrangement. But, you'll have to let me know when you feel I'm being too demanding.

Exercise Module 16

Model Responses for Situation 1

You: Tom/Terry, I need to sit down and have a discussion with you. I feel you've been too demanding of me lately.
Spouse/Boy/Girl: I don't understand.
You: Well, you always want me to drop whatever I'm doing and do what you want.
Spouse/Boy/Girl: We must have a misunderstanding.
You: All I know is, you're always having me do one thing or another for you at your convenience. I'd like you to be more considerate of my time.
Spouse/Boy/Girl: I really appreciate you, so I'm not sure I really understand.
You: Well, I don't always feel that you appreciate me. Even if you do, I can't spend all my time doing whatever you want. I need some time to do what I want, and also sometimes I'd like you to do what I want.
Spouse/Boy/Girl: Okay, we'll have to work out a better arrangement. But, you'll have to let me know when you feel I'm being too demanding.

Situation 2 – Expressing Personal Opinions

Your spouse/boyfriend/girlfriend says he/she wants you to visit a group of people for whom you do not care. You feel this particular group is immature and, at times, quite cold. You prefer not to associate with them and want to express this to your spouse/boyfriend/girlfriend.

You: _____

Spouse/Boy/Girl: Oh, they don't mean anything by their actions.
You: _____

Spouse/Boy/Girl: You just don't know them well enough.
You: _____

Spouse/Boy/Girl: If you can make another suggestion for the evening, I'll try that.

Situation 3 – Expressing Justified Annoyance or Anger

Your spouse/boyfriend/girlfriend has a habit of belittling you in front of others. He/she thinks his/her comments are funny, but you do not. Your spouse/boyfriend/girlfriend has just insulted you again. He/she says to you in front of a group of people, "Hey, shut up, give the rest of us a chance." You take your spouse/boyfriend/girlfriend aside and say:

You: _____

Spouse/Boy/Girl: What did I say?

You: _____

Spouse/Boy/Girl: No one paid any attention to that.

You: _____

Spouse/Boy/Girl: I guess I shouldn't say those things in front of everybody, but your behavior was really bothering me.

Situation 4 – Expressing Liking, Love, or Affection

You really like/love your spouse/boyfriend/girlfriend. However, you rarely express these feelings. You know how much you like it when your spouse/boyfriend/girlfriend expresses his/her affection to you. You're sitting in a quiet living room and want to tell your spouse/boyfriend/girlfriend how you feel about him/her.

You: _____

Spouse/Boy/Girl: Oh!

You: _____

Spouse/Boy/Girl: I feel the same about you.

Exercise Module 16

Writing Your Own Practice Situations and Deciding on Homework Assignments

After you have practiced the above situations, you can write some personal situations that involve asserting yourself with your partner. You should develop situations that are likely to occur in your daily interactions and in which you feel you could use some practice. These situations also may be related to the homework assignments that you plan to try out in your environment. Remember, the main point of all the practice is to help you to express yourself in real-life interactions.

On the next two pages, space is provided to develop your own situations to practice. Space also is provided to jot down homework assignments.

Personal Situation—Assertion in Couples

Describe Situation: _____
_____
_____

You: _____
_____

Other Person: _____
_____

You: _____
_____

Other Person: _____
_____

You: _____
_____

Personal Situation—Assertion in Couples

Describe Situation: _____
_____
_____

You: _____
_____

Other Person: _____
_____

You: _____
_____

Other Person: _____
_____

You: _____
_____

Exercise Module 16

Homework Assignment

List some possible situations in which you could practice asserting yourself with your partner. After you complete your list, star * a few you would like to being with. Choose one for your first assignment. You may find it helpful to rehearse your homework assignments before you try your new behavior in your daily interactions. Remember to start out with easy assignments first, and remember both to evaluate (criteria card in Discussion Module 4) and record (Tables 3 and 4) your behavior.

1.

2.

3.

4.

5.

6.

Discussion Module **17**

Assertion in Work Situations

This module contains material that is relevant to asserting yourself with business and professional colleagues, co-workers, and subordinates. Obviously, assertion in work situations also involves being able to express yourself to supervisors and bosses. However, these individuals represent authority figures, and issues related to coping with authorities are presented in Discussion Module 15.

Assertion in work settings is affected by the fact that personal communication occurs within an organizational setting and therefore often is complicated by organizational structure, policies, and procedures. Personal communication is overlaid with business and professional jargon, bureaucratic red tape, and unwritten codes of behavior. Through unwritten codes of behavior, secretaries learn that it is not acceptable to fraternize or express themselves openly with top executives but that having coffee with middle-management people is permissable. Executives who are on the rise quickly learn that their time is better spent conversing with their superiors rather than their subordinates. In addition, communication often flows through chains of command, by appointment, and by office memoranda rather than from person to person. The result is that much of the communication process is formalized, and barriers are placed even between individuals who occupy similar positions within the organization. Thus, much of the communication between people becomes indirect rather than direct. The problems with indirect communication have been discussed earlier. In summary they include the increased possibility of misinterpretation, the difficulty of determining intent, and the development of a sense of distance between people. In many ways, an organizational structure does little to encourage and much to discourage assertive behavior among its members.

Given the restrictions of the setting and the fact that most people will not be able to significantly alter institutional requirements, assertion will require a more concerted effort on your part than in some other settings. Asserting yourself in this setting may help prevent the development of feeling unappreciated and taken for granted, an experience that is all too common in large organizations.

It is particularly important in work situations to communicate clearly and specifically. For example, if you and a colleague are collaborating on a project, it is important to specify clearly the duties of each person as well as the meeting times that are involved. This specification will help to eliminate the frustration and institutional buck passing that can occur when clear responsibility for completing a task is not established.

In work settings, positive and negative feedback must be provided if tasks are to be accomplished on a continuous basis. Therefore, it is beneficial to be able to express and respond to both positive and negative feelings. If you work closely with people over a period of time, it is important to compliment them and express appreciation when it is justified. Such expressions build closer working relationships and reduce the likelihood that others will feel taken for granted. Similarly, it is important to be able to receive positive feelings gracefully. Denying or taking exception to a compliment indicates to the person giving the compliment that you consider his/her judgment to be faulty or that he/she is insincere. Such behavior will do little to strengthen the working relationship between the two of you.

Negative feelings often are more difficult to express and to respond to than positive feelings. However, the ability to cope with these feelings is necessary in most work situations. Being able to express negative feelings such as criticism and displeasure when they occur reduces the likelihood that these feelings will build up and undermine the working relationship.

Giving criticism and expressing annoyance assertively involves taking responsibility for and owning the displeasure or criticism; labeling the specific behavior with which you are displeased; clearly indicating what you would like changed the next time; and avoiding name calling, threats, and insults. By expressing displeasure in this manner, you minimize the possibility that your colleague or subordinate will react to your message as a personal attack on his/her competence. Evaluation is an integral part of every job, but it is important to direct the evaluation to the performance and not to the person.

Responding to critical evaluation (criticism) assertively involves reacting to it directly and honestly. The first step is to assess the criticism as objectively as possible to determine whether it is justified. If it is justified, you can decide whether a change in your behavior is indicated. Close and effective working relationships involve a mutual give and take that is facilitated by assertive behavior. This give and take also includes the skill of self-affirmation. Being able to stand up for your rights often prevents you from being manipulated by bosses, colleagues, or subordinates into taking on more than your fair share of the work.

Listed below are some of the common misconceptions and counterproductive beliefs concerning assertion in work situations and internal dialogues for disputing them. Discussion Module 3 contains some additional suggestions for changing these counterproductive beliefs.

Counterproductive beliefs about rights and responsibilities

I really don't have the right to ask my subordinate to come on time, to leave on time, and to do a competent job since he/she is having such severe personal and family problems. Anyway, two months is not such a long time to be inconvenienced.

Why is this so? Sure, most bosses like to be understanding and give their employees a break when they're having tough times. But, am I giving this person a break, or am I being used? I have the right to expect acceptable performance on the job. I need not feel guilty for expecting it. I've been understanding, but it seems as if this person is playing on my sympathies at this point.

Counterproductive beliefs about how I should behave or appear to others

If I ask for help or information from my co-workers, I'll appear incompetent. If worse comes to worse, I'll do the job over.

Why is this so? I can't be expected to know everything. People ask me for help now and then, don't they? Besides, it seems foolish to consider repeating the task instead of just asking for help. I have a right to ask for help if I need it.

It's easier for me to do my work and my colleague's as well than to ask him/her to do his/her fair share. If word gets around that I'm making demands on him/her, people will think that I can't handle the work.

This belief doesn't help me to avoid significant unpleasantness without denying my rights. I don't like having to do all the work when it is both of our responsibility. I'm being taken advantage of. I can't control what other people think. I have the right to expect that the other person do his/her part. Confronting my colleague may not be easy, but it will help me get my work finished and home on time.

Counterproductive or erroneous beliefs about probable consequences

I don't have to tell my staff that they are doing a good job. They are getting paid for it and will do a good job regardless of what I say.

Is this true? How did I feel when I was in their position? I enjoyed hearing positive comments about my work regardless of whether I was being well paid. A compliment every now and then made me feel better about myself and how I was handling my job. It seemed to motivate me. I can see that it is important for me to express appreciation to people if I feel they deserve it.

EXERCISE MODULE 17
SITUATIONS TO PRACTICE ASSERTION
IN WORK SITUATIONS

Four situations are provided in this module for you to practice asserting yourself in work situations. In addition to these situations, situations dealing with work interactions are provided in Exercise Module 5, Situation 1; Exercise Module 6, Situation 2; and Exercise Module 12, Situation 2. Work situations involving assertion with authority figures (for example, bosses and supervisors) will be found in Exercise Module 6, Situation 3; Exercise Module 12, Situation 1; and Exercise Module 15, Situations 3 and 4.

Each situation in this exercise module is labeled with the type of behavior called for, such as expressing legitimate rights, giving a compliment, and so on. If you have difficulty with a situation, read the discussion module dealing with the particular behavior under consideration.

In each situation provided for you to practice, the comments of the other person are not always assertive. However, your task is to be assertive in your comments. In addition, model assertive responses for "you" are given for Situation 1. Remember to practice each situation as many times as you feel it is necessary. Also use the summary sheet on pages 77-78 when practicing the situations and evaluating your behavior. Finally, you are to design your own situations to practice and develop a list of real life situations to use as homework assignments.

Situation 1–Expressing Justified Annoyance or Displeasure

You are a supervisor, and one of your employees has been consistently late for work during the past two weeks. You have called the employee into your office to discuss the situation with him/her.

You: _____

Employee: But I couldn't help it. I overslept.

You: _____

Employee: Fifteen or twenty minutes doesn't really make a difference, does it?

You: _____

Employee: I've seen other employees come in late.

You: _____

Employee: Okay, I'll try to do better.

Model Responses for Situation 1

You: Don/Donna. I called you in to talk about the fact that you have been coming late to work these past two weeks.
Employee: But I couldn't help it. I overslept.
You: I haven't been pleased by your lateness, and I expect you to be on time in the future.
Employee: Fifteen or twenty minutes doesn't really make a difference, does it?
You: I feel it does.
Employee: I've seen other employees come in late.
You: We're talking about your behavior. I want you to be on time from now on.
Employee: Okay, I'll try to do better.

Reminder: Get right to the point. Don't engage in unnecessary formalities. Don't get sidetracked by your employee. You need not discuss the behavior of other employees.

Situation 2 – Refusing a Request

You are up to your ears in work. You cannot take on any new tasks at this point. One of your co-workers is approaching you now to ask for assistance with his/her job.

Co-worker: Walt/Wendi, I'm really busy and need someone to cover for me during lunch break. I'm supposed to watch over things then.
You: _____

Co-worker: *Please*, just this time.
You: _____

Co-worker: You're not that busy.
You: _____

Reminder: You need not feel guilty. You can't be helpful all the time. At times you have to consider your own needs.

Situation 3 – Expressing Justified Annoyance or Displeasure

Your co-workers always seem to be teasing you about one thing or another—your new outfits, what you're planning to do, and so on. You're tired of being teased. You have decided the next time it occurs to express your annoyance and request that it doesn't occur again.

Co-worker: Hey, look at your new shoes. Where do you think you're going? To see the President?

You: _____
_____

Co-worker: Can't you take a little joke?

You: _____
_____

Co-worker: Well, I'll cut it out if it bothers you.

Situation 4 – Giving a Compliment

One of your co-workers has been quite helpful. He/she completed many of the tasks you fell behind on when you were sick. He/she didn't have to do this for you, but you certainly felt relieved to find that your work was up to date when you returned. You want to express your appreciation.

You: _____
_____

Co-worker: It was the least I could do.

You: _____
_____

Co-worker: I know how it can be to miss a week at work. I'm glad I could be of help.

You: _____
_____

Writing Your Own Practice Situations and Deciding on Homework Assignments

After you have practiced the above situations, you can write some personal situations that involve asserting yourself in work situations. You should develop situations that are likely to occur in your daily interactions and in which you feel you could use some practice. These situations also may be related to the homework assignments that you plan to try out in your environment. Remember, the main point of all the practice is to help you to express yourself in real-life interactions.

On the next two pages, space is provided to develop your own situations to practice. Space also is provided to jot down homework assignments.

Personal Situation—Assertion in Work Situations

Describe Situation: _____
_____
_____

You: _____
_____

Other Person: _____
_____

You: _____
_____

Other Person: _____
_____

You: _____
_____

Personal Situation—Assertion in Work Situations

Describe Situation: _____
_____
_____

You: _____
_____

Other Person: _____
_____

You: _____
_____

Other Person: _____
_____

You: _____
_____

Homework Assignment

List some possible situations in which you could practice assertion in work situations. After you complete your list, star * a few you would like to begin with. Choose one for your first assignment. You may find it helpful to rehearse your homework assignments before you try your new behavior in your daily interactions. Remember to start out with easy assignments first, and remember both to evaluate (criteria card in Discussion Module 4) and record (Tables 3 and 4) your behavior.

1.

2.

3.

4.

5.

6.

Discussion Module **18**

Assertion for College Students

The college years present students with a number of developmental tasks of life to master. These tasks have important implications for assertive behavior. In many ways, the college years involve the resolution of the problems and concerns of adolescence.*

One important task of your adolescent and college years is the readjustment of the relationship with your parents from that of a child-parent to an adult-adult relationship. In the child-parent relationship you are dependent on your parents to make decisions for you and are obligated to comply with those decisions. In the adult-adult relationship, you are independent and make decisions for yourself, perhaps with consultation from other adults such as your parents. During the college years, the relationship between you and your parents is in a state of transition, a state that can be somewhat uncomfortable for both sides as you begin to assert your in-independence and as your parents begin to adjust to it.

One issue that can complicate the relationship is the fact that many college students often are financially dependent on their parents even though they are independent in other ways. Often the financial dependence is used by parents as a means to control or postpone emotional independence—"We still pay your bills. If we want you to come home on the weekend, you had better think seriously about the consequences of not complying with our request." What is called for here is negotiation about exactly what emotional strings are attached to financial support so that constant threat or withdrawal of support does not occur each time you assert your independence. If you are aware of the conditions under which

---
*F.W. Coons, "The Resolution of Adolescence in College," *The Personnel and Guidance Journal* 7 (1970), 533-541.

chapter 5: Assertion in Special Situations and with Special People

the money is given, then you can decide whether the emotional price is too high to pay. We refer you to Discussion Module 14 for additional issues concerning assertion with parents.

A second task involves your development as an independent adult in general. For many people, the college years are the first time that they have full control over their lives. This control includes such relatively straightforward matters as learning to schedule one's time and to determine one's hours as well as more complex matters such as developing and expressing one's opinions on politics, personal preferences, and a philosophy of life. As a result, the ability to express your personal opinions becomes increasingly important during the college years (see Discussion Module 11).

Another task concerns developing the capacity for close and/or intimate relationships with same or opposite sex peers. College may present you with the first opportunity to live with someone other than a brother/sister with whom you have grown up. In such a situation, successful adjustment involves the ability to assert personal preferences and to compromise if different living habits or lifestyles are encountered. For example, you like to study with the radio on, and your rommmate likes to study with it off. You like to go to sleep by 11:00, and your roommate is a night owl. You like the room to be relatively neat, but your roommate couldn't care less about neatness. To withhold your opinion on these matters undoubtedly would result in considerable discomfort for you. In the past if you were dissatisfied with the living habits of the brother/sister with whom you shared a room, you could speak to your parents and count on them to intervene. Now it is up to you. You have the choice of speaking up and possibly risking your roommate's displeasure (short-term consequences) or of saying nothing and being unhappy all semester (long-term consequences) while hoping that your roommate will read your mind and comply with your wishes. Asserting yourself increases the likelihood that your preferences will be respected or that some form of compromise will be reached.

Developing the capacity for intimate relationships with the opposite sex is a particularly important developmental task during the college years, since many of the relationships that are formed during this period turn out to be relatively enduring. Intimacy goes beyond sexual encounters. It involves mutual give and take and the ability to assert yourself about positive feelings, negative feelings, and personal rights as the relationship requires. If a relationship is truly intimate, then both parties feel free to assert themselves without fear that the relationship will dissolve as a consequence. For example, if you have a preference about either the amount of time you spend together or your personal freedom, then you have the right to express this preference. Similarly, if you feel that you are not interested in a sexual encounter on a particular occasion or at a particular point in the relationship, then you can assert this preference without having to worry that the other person will feel rejected or that you are violating the rules of conduct for relationships with the opposite sex.

Another task that you may encounter is that of a change in your role as a student. In some ways, college will encourage you to take on the role of an independent, inquiring scholar rather than a passive recipient of knowledge. You may find that your professors, unlike your high school teachers, encourage and even require you to question traditional points of view and to initiate conversations and raise questions in class discussions. If you find that you have difficulty in expressing personal opinions, you may want to read Discussion Module 11.

A final task concerns modification in the nature of the relationship with authority figures. The ways in which these relationships are modified is typified by the changes in the student-instructor relationship from high school to college. In high school, your instructor had the power to discipline as well as the power of academic evaluation and superiority of knowledge over you. But, as you become an adult, much of the power to discipline that typified relationships between authority figures and children is increasingly absent from the relationship between instructor/authority figures and you as a young adult. You should begin to recognize that you have the right to be treated fairly and as a person with rights equal to those of the authority. Questioning an authority about a decision or a point of view is acceptable from an adult (college student), whereas it might be regarded as defiance from a child. It often is this fear of defying an authority and of subsequent punishment left over from childhood that prevents many college students from raising legitimate concerns in an appropriate manner with instructors and other college authorities.

The majority of the counterproductive beliefs and attitudes that college students and other adults adhere to have been mentioned in previous discussion modules. In particular, we refer you to the discussion modules dealing with expressing personal opinions, expressing legitimate rights, and assertion with parents, assertion with authorities, and assertion in couples. In addition to the counterproductive attitudes discussed in other modules, we present below two counterproductive attitudes that are particularly relevant to college students.

Counterproductive beliefs about rights and responsibilities

I am still young and naive and don't have the right to my own point of view yet. Furthermore, I'm not really responsible for my words and actions. I'm only a kid.

Why is this so? Would this position stand up in a court of law? Of course not. I am an adult, and I have the right to my own opinions even though they may not be backed up with as much experience as those of someone else. I also am responsible. By saying that I'm not responsible, am I really saying that I'm afraid to be an adult and that I don't think that I'm ready to assume those responsibilities? I am an adult whether I like it or not, and being an adult gives me both rights and responsibilities.

Counterproductive or erroneous beliefs about probable consequences

I am an adult. People should recognize this and treat me as an adult. They should respect my rights and give me the consequences I desire . . . (or else).

This belief certainly doesn't help me to achieve my goals and to do so without hurting others. When I hear myself saying such things, I guess I sound aggressive and uncompromising. I sound more like a child than an adult when I behave this way. I do have a right to assert my point of view and to express my annoyance if people don't treat me as an adult. I don't have the right to force them to do what I want.

EXERCISE MODULE 18
SITUATIONS TO PRACTICE ASSERTION
FOR COLLEGE STUDENTS

Six situations are provided for you to practice asserting yourself. These are situations with which college students are often confronted. Many of the situations in Exercise Modules 5 through 17 are also applicable to college students. Particularly relevant situations include Situation 4 in Exericse Module 5; Situation 3 in Exercise Module 6; Situation 1 in Exercise Module 10; Situation 2 in Exericse Module 12; and Situation 2 in Exercise Module 15.

Each situation in this exercise module is labeled with the type of behavior called for, for example, expressing legitimate rights, and giving a compliment. If you have difficulty with a situation, read the discussion module dealing with the particular behavior under consideration.

In each situation provided for you to practice, the comments of the other person are not always assertive. However, your task is to be assertive in your comments. In addition, model assertive responses for "you" are given for Situation 1. Remember to practice each situation as many times as you feel it is necessary. Also use the summary sheet on pages 77-78 when practicing the situations and evaluating your behavior. Finally, you are to design your own situations to practice and develop a list of real-life situations to use as homework assignments.

Situation 1–Refusing a Request

You have a term paper due in three days and really want to work on it this evening. You have purposely gone to the library so you wouldn't be interrupted. You have just started writing when your friend comes up and asks you to join him/her for a movie. You know you want to work on your paper.

Friend: Hi Mel/Maggie. How about going to a good movie with me now?

You: _____

Friend: Is it due tomorrow?

You: _____

Friend: Then come on. You have plenty of time to do it.

You: _____

Friend: Don't be that way. Hard work won't get you anywhere.

You: _____

Friend: This is the last night the movie will be showing.

You: _____

Friend: Okay then.

Model Responses for Situation 1

Friend:	Hi, Mel/Maggie. How about going to a good movie with me now?
You:	Not tonight. I have a paper to write.
Friend:	Is it due tomorrow?
You:	No, in three days.
Friend:	Then come on. You have plenty of time to do it.
You:	I want to work on it tonight.
Friend:	Don't be that way. Hard work won't get you anywhere.
You:	Not tonight.
Friend:	This is the last night the movie will be showing.
You:	Not this time. I want to get some work done. Thanks for asking.
Friend:	Okay then.

Reminder: You need not make up excuses for wanting to do your paper ahead of time. You have a right to study when you want to. If your friend persists, you need to repeat your comments in a firm and definitive manner.

Situation 2 – Making a Request

You are expecting a very important phone call between 7 and 10 P.M. tonight. You also have a class to attend from 7 to 8:30. You know your roommate is planning to remain in the dorm tonight. You want to ask him/her to listen to the phone and take a message if the call comes in before you get back.

You: _____

Roommate: I'm not sure if I'll be here all night.
You: _____

Roommate: That will be about two hours.
You: _____

Roommate: They'll probably call back.
You: _____

Roomate: Okay, I'll listen for the phone while I'm studying.

Situation 3 – Expressing Liking and Affection

You went to a party with your boyfriend/girlfriend. Although the party was very dull, you still enjoyed yourself because you enjoy being with your date. You and your date are saying goodnight. You want him/her to know that you enjoyed being with him/her.

Date: That wasn't a very good party.
You: _____

Date: My friends are usually a lot more lively.
You: _____

Date: Thanks, but I hope the next party is better.

214   chapter 5: Assertion in Special Situations and with Special People

Situation 4 – Expressing Justified Annoyance

You have a car, and many of your friends do not. You have let them use your car a number of times. Today when you came back to your room, you noticed that the extra set of keys is missing. You check on your car and see that it's gone. You look again and find a note in your desk that says, "I had to pick up a package. Thanks. Bob/Barbara." You are quite annoyed by this and feel you are being taken advantage of. Here comes your friend with the keys now.

Friend: Here are the keys. Thanks.

You: _____

Friend: I wasn't gone long.

You: _____

Friend: You would have let me use it if I asked. You wouldn't have said no.

You: _____

Reminder: Be careful not to end your conversation by agreeing with your friend that you would have let him/her use your car if you were there. Whether you would have granted permission or not is irrelevant. You need to make it clear that you feel your friend's behavior was unacceptable.

Situation 5 – Expressing Personal Opinions

In class today your professor made a number of comments about today's youth. You disagree with his/her views, and have some additional points you'd like to discuss with him/her. You are outside his/her office.

Professor: Come in.

You: _____

Professor: What do you mean?

You: _____

Professor: I'm not sure I've heard of those views before.

You: _____

Professor: It's good to hear what our students feel about these issues. I'm glad you took the time to come by.

Exercise Module 18

Situation 6–Standing Up for Your Rights

You are attending a sporting event this evening with a few friends. You've been looking forward to this evening for some time. As you are leaving your house, your mom/dad says "I'll see you right after the game." However, you hadn't planned on coming home immediately.

Parent: See you after the game.

You: _____

Parent: The game only lasts a couple of hours.

You: _____

Parent: There's no reason to run around town and get into trouble.

You: _____

Parent: I don't want you out all night.

You: _____

Parent: Okay then, don't make it too late.

Writing Your Own Practice Situations and Deciding on Homework Assignments

After you have practiced the above situations, you can write some personal situations that involve assertions by college students. You should develop situations that are likely to occur in your daily interactions and in which you feel you could use some practice. These situations also may be related to the homework assignments that you plan to try out in your environment. Remember, the main point of all the practice is to help you to express yourself in real-life interactions.

On the next two pages, space is provided to develop your own situations to practice. Space is also provided to jot down homework assignments.

Personal Situation—Assertion by College Students

Describe Situation: _____
_____
_____

You: _____
_____

Other Person: _____
_____

You: _____
_____

Other Person: _____
_____

You: _____
_____

Personal Situation—Assertion by College Students

Describe Situation: _____
_____
_____

You: _____
_____

Other Person: _____
_____

You: _____
_____

Other Person: _____
_____

You: _____
_____

Homework Assignment

List some possible situations in which you could practice asserting yourself in college situations. After you complete your list, star * a few you would like to begin with. Choose one for your first assignment in this area. You may find it helpful to rehearse your homework assignments before you try your new behavior in your daily interactions. Remember to start out with easy assignments first, and remember both to evaluate (criteria card in Discussion Module 4) and record (Tables 3 and 4) your behavior.

1.

2.

3.

4.

5.

6.

Chapter 6

Concluding Remarks

Throughout this manual, we have provided a number of procedures, suggestions, and exercises to help you assess and modify both attitudes and behaviors that are relevant to self-assertion. Those of you who have systematically completed your assertion training program at this point undoubtedly have made important and significant changes in the way you think about and relate to other people. Those of you who are about to begin your programs can look forward to such changes following a good bit of hard work. Assertion training is not a panacea. It does not guarantee that people automatically will flock to you, that your personality will change radically, or that all your problems will suddenly disappear. However, it can provide you with a new and important set of communication skills and another way to view yourself and your relationships with other people.

As we have mentioned before, assertion training is not a method for getting what you want from your environment regardless of the cost to others. Rather, it is a way of making your needs, opinions, rights, and feelings known in an appropriate manner so that there will be little misunderstanding about where you stand and how you feel. We believe that people generally feel better about themselves and have greater self-respect if they are able to directly communicate how they feel about an issue than if they feel too inhibited to speak or if they can only communicate in indirect ways by having to qualify or apologize for everything they say. As we have said before, indirect or implied communication is annoying to have to decipher, often forces the listener to be a mind reader, and is subject to misinterpretation. If you communicate clearly and directly, it is not likely that you will be misunderstood. We believe that such communication increases the probability that your opinions will be respected and that your interactions with others will work out favorably both from your perspective and that of the other person.

Assertion does not occur in a vacuum. It has consequences for you and for others in your environment. By this time, we trust that you have developed the ability to make responsible judgments about how you will behave in a situation based on an evaluation of your needs, rights, and responsibilities; the other person's rights and responsibilities; and the expected short- and long-term consequences of the possible courses of action open to you in the situation.

Remember that in any situation *you choose* how you will behave. This book has provided you with the procedures for developing the ability to assert yourself as well as the considerations involved in choosing to assert yourself. However, the final decision to behave assertively or not in a given situation *is always up to you*.

Good luck with your future assertions. You have the *right* to express your feelings, preferences, needs, and opinions without excessive anxiety or guilt and the *responsibility* to express these in a way that does not threaten, insult, or hurt other people.

Appendix A
Additional Trainer Considerations: Assertion for Children

Although this manual was not designed specifically for use with children, assertive behavior is an important skill for children to learn. It is likely that with modifications and simplifications, a trainer could apply the general strategies and approaches presented in this manual to develop assertion training programs for children.

One of the first modifications needed would be in the assessment procedures which were described in Exercise Module 1. Table 6 is an Assertion Assessment Table for Children. It is likely that the table could be completed by some older children or adolescents working by themselves. Others would require assistance from adults. For a young child, a person who knows the child well and has the opportunity to observe him/her in a variety of situations could complete the inventory for the child or in conjunction with the child. It is important for the observer who completes the inventory to have a good understanding of what is appropriate social behavior for children of different age groups.

The importance of different portions of the table will vary depending on the age of the child. For example, the columns marked *Friends of Same Sex* and *Friends of Opposite Sex* will take on different significance at different ages. Another change that would have to be made is to simplify the language on the criteria card and to train much more slowly, being careful to stress only a few behaviors and certainly only one behavior at a time. It would seem particularly important to help children to look at the other person and to say exactly what it is that they want to say and perhaps to sacrifice some of the other nonverbal behaviors and perhaps some of the paralanguage behaviors for the sake of simplicity. It is important for children to learn to say what they feel so that they don't learn to be inhibited at an early age.

From our perspective, assertion training would seem particularly helpful for the shy, "shrinking violet" child. This child could profit from learning skills concerned with initiating and maintaining conversations as a way of helping him/her to develop new friendships with other children. Learning to say "nice things" to other children would be another behavior that would be helpful in developing new relationships. In addition, he/she might find it very helpful to learn to stand up for legitimate rights and to express justified annoyance and anger. Often, it

Table 6
Assertion Assessment Table for Children

Behaviors	Friends of the same sex	Friends of the opposite sex	Parents	Brother(s) and Sister(s)	Authority figures, e.g. teachers, principals	Business contacts, e.g. salespersons, waiters
Expressing Positive Feelings						
Give compliments						
Receive compliments						
Make requests, e.g. ask for favors, help, etc.						
Express liking, love, and affection						
Initiate and maintain conversations						
Self-Affirmation						
Stand up for your legitimate rights						
Refuse requests						
Express personal opinions including disagreement						
Expressing Negative Feelings						
Express justified annoyance and displeasure						
Express justified anger						

Instructions for Assertion Assessment Table for Children

1. Do I (row heading) to/from/of/with (column heading) when it is appropriate? usually   sometimes   seldom
2. When I (row heading) to/from/of/with (column heading) do I become very nervous or unduly anxious? yes   no
3. Am I aggressive when I (row heading) to/from/of/with (column heading)? If you respond yes, shade that cell.

Appendix A

is the shy child who is victimized by the local bully and whose rights generally are ignored by others. When the child's rights are ignored, he/she can't help feeling badly about himself/herself. This lack of self-esteem, in turn, can result in a lack of confidence by the child in his/her ability to interact successfully with peers which leads to further isolation and retardation in the development of social skills. Thus, teaching the child to assert himself/herself can result in interrupting the low self-esteem/withdrawal cycle that is often characteristic of shy children.

Assertion training also is of potential relevance for the child whose behavior is characterized by frequent aggression and bullying of others. Such a child could profit from learning more about the rights of others and about socially appropriate ways to express his/her needs and feelings.

Handling consumer situations is an area in which children can learn to assert themselves as they are growing up. All consumers regardless of age, sex, or race should have the same rights. If a child is spending his/her money for an item, he/she has the right to get what he/she wants; the right to fair treatment; the right not to have to wait until a group of adults who have come in after him/her are served; and the right not to be ripped off because he/she is not as sophisticated a consumer as most adults. We believe that it is important for children not to feel intimidated by consumer interactions.

It is important to bear in mind several cautions when using assertion training with children. First, assertive behavior may not be welcomed and even may be punished by adults. For example, there is a body of educational research which indicates that school personnel value and reward the docile child and punish the child who displays curiosity and what may be labelled assertive behavior. As a result, you might want to be cautious about teaching a child to engage in assertive behavior with his/her teacher. You certainly will want to alert the child to the fact that some adults might not like his/her assertive behavior and prepare him/her for the possible negative consequences, such as verbal reprimand. It is the area of expressing negative feelings and to a lesser extent the areas of standing up for legitimate rights and expressing personal opinions that might result in unfavorable reactions from adults. It is desirable to teach children to distinguish between behavior which is appropriately assertive with adults whom they know well (like parents) as opposed to adults they don't know well. A consultation with the child's parents is recommended in order to determine which behaviors they will encourage and reward and which behaviors they will not. In this way, the child can learn to adapt his/her behavior to the situation in which he/she finds himself/herself or at least to recognize that certain behaviors may be rewarded within the home but may be punished outside the home.

Another important issue concerns the identification of legitimate rights for children. It is unquestionable that children have the right to be treated fairly and with respect. Beyond this, however, the area of children's legitimate rights can be somewhat fuzzy, particularly in situations in which adults are involved. It is obvious that a three-year-old does not have the same rights as an adult. He/she does not, for example, have the right to decide to cross a busy street for himself/herself. How about a seventeen-year-old? Obviously, he/she has this right. We believe that a person's rights are determined to a large extent by the skills he/she possesses and the extent to which he/she can be expected to take on the responsibilities that accompany his/her behavior. As a child becomes older and develops more skills and the capability to assume increasing responsibility, we grant him/her more and more rights. Hopefully, this transition is a smooth one that is tailored to the ability of each child.

Unfortunately, many parents and other adults are reluctant to grant the child his/her rights, thereby forcing the child to prove to the adult that he/she has the skills and can assume the responsibilities that go with those rights. In teaching a child to be assertive about legitimate rights, it is important that he/she realize that he/she may not be ready to assume the right and/or that the adult may be either unwilling to grant the right or to listen to the child's point of view. Of course, the child has a right to his/her point of view. However, he/she may feel justifiably annoyed if the adult won't listen to it. In such situations, assertion training, particularly with an emphasis on rights, is needed not only for the child but for significant adults such as parents, teachers, and scout leaders in his/her environment.

We feel that the most important use of assertion training for children is in teaching them to relate effectively to their peers. Once again, a caution must be observed. Teaching children to relate effectively to their peers involves teaching them behavior that is appropriate and adaptive for their age and cultural groups. It is important to determine what is appropriate behavior either through observation or through consultation with some of the child's peers who are recognized as being assertive in the peer group. Failure to do this runs the risk of teaching a child behavior that will be mocked or punished by his/her peers, thereby increasing the social distance between the child and his/her peers.

Situations for Children

A number of situations are provided that are appropriate for children. Of course, depending on the child's age, some modifications may be needed. If you are working with teenagers, especially high school students, some of the situations for college students may be appropriate with slight changes in the wording. Throughout the book, there are many other situations that could be modified and used with children.

Situation 1–Expressing Personal Opinions in Class

Your class is discussing the family. Your teacher made a comment about how families use their time together. You want to tell how your family uses its time and why you think it is a good way to use its time.

Teacher: Many families like to spend Sundays together.

You: _____

Teacher: Could you tell us more about that?

You: _____

Teacher: That's another way that families can spend their time.

Situation 2–Making a Request of a Peer

You have some children you play with at school, but there are not many children in your neighborhood. Your parents said you could invite someone from your class to your house for the afternoon and to stay for dinner. You want to invite one of your classmates to your house.

You: _____

Friend: When?
You: _____

Friend: I'd like to, but I'll have to check with my mom.
You: _____

Situation 3–Expressing Justified Annoyance or Displeasure

Another child in your class keeps going into your desk and taking your pencils. You've seen this boy/girl go into your desk a number of times. As you walk into your room after recess, you see this boy/girl at your desk taking your pencil again. You decide to tell him/her that you don't want him/her doing this again.

You: _____

Classmate: I was just looking at it.
You: _____

Classmate: I didn't do that.
You: _____

Classmate: Okay, I'll stay away from your desk.

Situation 4 – Giving a Compliment

One of your friends has made a really clever poster. You want to tell him/her that you really like it.

You: _____

Friend: Oh, it's just a poster.

You: _____

Friend: Thanks, I'm glad you like it.

Situation 5 – Initiating and Maintaining a Conversation

A new boy/girl about your age has just moved two doors away. You want to meet him/her.

You: _____

New Neighbor: Hi, I'm Gary/Gail.

You: _____

New Neighbor: That sounds like fun.

You: _____

Hints: Suggest to the child an opening such as, "Hi, I'm _____. I live down the street." You can also suggest that he/she asks the other child about his/her interests or ask the new neighbor such questions as, "Where did you live before?" "What grade are you in?" "Do you have any brothers or sisters?"

Appendix A

Situation 6 – Standing Up for Your Rights

You have made plans to play with some children today. As you're putting on your jacket, your mom says that she wants you to rake the leaves right now. You don't mind doing it and you do get paid, but you already have plans. You want to do it tomorrow. You need to speak to your mom about this.

Mom: Paul/Pam, I want you to rake the leaves before you go out.

You: _____

Mom: Look, I want it done now. You get paid. What else do you want?

You: _____

Mom: When will you get to it? This is one job I depend on you for.

You: _____

Mom: Okay, but don't forget.

Hints: A situation such as this one may only be profitable to practice if you know or believe that the parents would be reasonable if their child stood up for his/her rights. You do not want the child to be punished for asserting that his/her time and plans are also important. Negotiation is obviously needed here.

Appendix B
Principles for Ethical Practice of Assertive Behavior Training *

With the increasing popularity of assertive behavior training, a quality of faddishness has become evident, and there are frequent reports of ethically irresponsible practices (and practitioners). We hear of trainers who, for example, do not adequately differentiate assertion and aggression. Others have failed to advocate proper ethical responsibility and caution to clients—for example, failed to alert them to and/or prepare them for the possibility of retaliation or other highly negative reactions from others.

The following statement of principles for ethical practice of assertive behavior training is the work of the professional psychologists and educators listed below, who are actively engaged in the practice of facilitating assertive behavior (also referred to as "assertive therapy," "social skills training," "personal effectiveness training," and "A-T"). We do not intend by this statement to discourage untrained individuals from becoming more assertive on their own, and we do not advocate that one must have extensive credentials in order to be of help to friends and relatives. Rather, these principles are offered to help foster responsible and ethical teaching and practice by human services professionals. Others who wish to enhance their own assertiveness or that of associates are encouraged to do so, with awareness of their own limitations, and of the importance of seeking help from a qualified therapist/trainer when necessary.

---

*Source: *Assert 8, The Newsletter of Assertive Behavior.* Impact Publishers, Inc., June 1976.

We hereby declare support for and adherence to the statement of principles, and invite responsible professionals in our own and other fields who use these techniques to join us in advocating and practicing these principles.

Robert E. Alberti
California Polytechnic State University
San Luis Obispo, CA

Michael L. Emmons
California Polytechnic State University
San Luis Obispo, CA

Iris G. Fodor
New York University, Washington Square
New York, NY

John P. Galassi
University of North Carolina
Chapel Hill, NC

Merna Dee Galassi
Meredith College
Raleigh, NC

Lynne Garnett
University of California
Los Angeles, CA

Patricia Jakubowski
University of Missouri
St. Louis, MO

Janet L. Wolfe
Institute for Advanced Study
in Rational Psychotherapy
New York, NY

1. **Definition of Assertive Behavior**

    For purposes of these principles and the ethical framework expressed herein, we define assertive behavior as that complex of behaviors emitted by a person in an interpersonal context which express that person's feelings, attitudes, wishes, opinions, or rights directly, firmly, and honestly, while respecting the feelings, attitudes, wishes, opinions, and rights of the other person(s). Such behavior may include the expression of such emotions as anger, fear, caring, hope, joy, despair, indignation, embarrassment, but in any event is expressed in a manner which does not violate the rights of others. Assertive behavior is differentiated from aggressive behavior which, while expressive of one person's feelings, attitudes, wishes, opinions, or rights, does not respect those characteristics in others.

    While this definition is intended to be comprehensive, it is recognized that any adequate definition of assertive behavior must consider several dimensions:

    A. *Intent*: Behavior classified as assertive is not intended by its author to be hurtful of others.
    B. *Behavior*: Behavior classified as assertive would be evaluated by an objective observer as itself honest, direct, expressive, and nondestructive of others.
    C. *Effects*: Behavior classified as assertive has the effect upon the receiver of a direct and nondestructive message, by which a "reasonable person" would not be hurt.
    D. *Sociocultural Context*: Behavior classified as assertive is appropriate to the environment and culture in which it is exhibited, and may not be considered assertive in a different sociocultural environment.

2. **Client Self-Determination**

    These principles recognize and affirm the inherent dignity and the equal and inalienable rights of all members of the human family, as proclaimed in the "Universal Declaration of Human Rights" endorsed by the General Assembly of the United Nations.

    Pursuant to the precepts of the Declaration, each client (trainee, patient) who seeks assertive behavior training shall be treated as a person of value, with all of the freedoms and rights expressed in the Declaration. No procedure shall be utilized in the name of assertive behavior training which would violate those freedoms or rights.

    Informed client self-determination shall guide all such interventions:

    A. The client shall be fully informed in advance of all procedures to be utilized
    B. The client shall have the freedom to choose to participate or not at any point in the intervention
    C. The client who is institutionalized shall be similarly treated with respect and without coercion, insofar as is possible within the institutional environment
    D. The client shall be provided with explicit definitions of assertiveness and assertion training
    E. The client shall be fully informed as to the education, training, experience or other qualifications of the assertive trainer(s)
    F. The client shall be informed as to the goals and potential outcomes of assertive training, including potentially high levels of anxiety and possible negative reactions from others.
    G. The client shall be fully informed as to the responsibility of the assertion trainer(s) and the client(s)
    H. The client shall be informed as to the ethics and employment of confidentiality guidelines as they pertain to various assertive training settings (for example, clinical versus nonclinical).

3. **Qualifications of Facilitators**

Assertive behavior training is essentially a therapeutic procedure, although frequently practiced in a variety of settings by professionals not otherwise engaged in rendering a "psychological" service. Persons in any professional role who engage in helping others to change their behavior, attitudes, and interpersonal relationships must understand human behavior at a level commensurate with the level of their interventions.

3.1 **General Qualifications**

We support the following minimum, general qualifications for facilitators at all levels of intervention (including "trainers in training"—preservice or inservice—who are preparing for professional service in a recognized human services field, and who may be conducting assertive behavior training under supervision as part of a research project or practicum):

A. Fundamental understanding of the principles of learning and behavior (equivalent to completion of a rigorous undergraduate level course in learning theory);

B. Fundamental understanding of anxiety and its effects upon behavior (equivalent to completion of a rigorous undergraduate level course in abnormal psychology);

C. Knowledge of the limitations, contraindications, and potential dangers of assertive behavior training; familiarity with theory and research in the area;

D. Satisfactory evidence of competent performance as a facilitator, as observed by a qualified trainer, is strongly recommended for all professionals, particularly for those who do not possess a doctorate or an equivalent level of training. Such evidence would most ideally be supported by:

1) participation in at least ten hours of assertive behavior training as a client (trainee, patient); and

2) participation in at least ten hours of assertive behavior training as a facilitator under supervision.

3.2 **Specific Qualifications**

The following additional qualifications are considered to be the minimum expected for facilitators at the indicated levels of intervention:

A. Assertive behavior training, including nonclinical workshops, groups, and individual client training aimed at teaching assertive skills to those persons who require only encouragement and specific skill training and in whom no serious emotional deficiency or pathology is evident.

1) For trainers in programs conducted under the sponsorship of a recognized human services agency, school, governmental or corporate entity, church, or community organization:

a) An advanced degree in a recognized field of human services (such as psychology, counseling, social work, medicine, public health, nursing, education, human development, theology/divinity), including at least one term of field experience in a human services agency supervised by a qualified trainer; or

b) Certification as a minister, public school teacher, social worker, physician, counselor, nurse, or clinical, counseling, educational, or school psychologist, or similar human services professional, as recognized by the state wherein employed or by the recognized state or national professional society in the indicated discipline; or

c) One year of paid counseling experience in a recognized human services agency, supervised by a qualified trainer; or

d) Qualification under items 3.2B or 3.2C below.

2) For trainers in programs including interventions at the level defined in this item

(3.2A), but without agency/organization sponsorship:
- a) An advanced degree in a recognized field of human services (such as psychology, counseling, social work, medicine, public health, nursing, education, human development, theology/divinity) including at least one term of field experience in a human services agency supervised by a qualified trainer; and
- b) Certification as a minister, social worker, physician, counselor, nurse, or clinical, counseling, educational, or school psychologist, or similar human services professional, as recognized by the state wherein employed or by the recognized state or national professional society in the indicated discipline; or
- c) Qualification under items 3.2B or 3.2C below.

B. Assertive behavior therapy, including clinical interventions designed to assist persons who are severely inhibited by anxiety, or who are significantly deficient in social skills, or who are controlled by aggression, or who evidence pathology, or for whom other therapeutic procedures are indicated:

1) For therapists in programs conducted under the sponsorship of a recognized human services agency, school, governmental or corporate entity, church, or community organization:
   - a) An advanced degree in a recognized field of human services (such as psychology, counseling, social work, medicine, public health, nursing, education, human development, theology/divinity) including at least one term of field experience in a human services agency supervised by a qualified trainer; or
   - b) Certification as a minister, social worker, physician, counselor, nurse, or clinical, counseling, educational, or school psychologist, as recognized by the state wherein employed or by the recognized state or national professional society in the individual discipline; or
   - c) Qualification under item 3.2C below.

2) For therapists employing interventions at the level defined in this item (3.2B), but without agency/organization sponsorship:
   - a) An advanced degree in a recognized field of human services (such as psychology, counseling, social work, medicine, public health, nursing, education, human development, theology/divinity) including at least one term of field experience in a human services agency supervised by a qualified trainer; and
   - b) Certification as minister, social worker, physician, counselor, nurse, or clinical, counseling, educational, or school psychologist, as recognized by the state wherein employed or by the recognized state or national professional society in the indicated discipline; and
   - c) At least one year of paid professional experience in a recognized human services agency, supervised by a qualified trainer; or
   - d) Qualification under item 3.2C below.

C. Training of trainers, including preparation of other professionals to offer assertive behavior training/therapy to clients, in school, agency, organization, or individual settings.

1) A doctoral degree in a recognized field of human services (such as psychology, counseling, social work, medicine, public health, nursing, education, human development, theology/divinity) including at least one term of field experience in a human services agency supervised by a qualified trainer; and

2) Certification as a minister, social worker, physician, counselor, nurse, or clinical, counseling, educational, or school psychologist, as recognized by the state wherein employed, or by the recognized state or national professional society in the indicated discipline; and

3) At least one year of paid professional experience in a recognized human services agency, supervised by a qualified trainer; and
4) Advanced study in assertive behavior training/therapy, including at least two of the following:
   a) At least thirty hours of facilitation with clients;
   b) Participation in at least two different workshops at professional meetings or professional training institutes;
   c) Contribution to the professional literature in the field.

3.3 We recognize that counselors and psychologists are not certified by each state. In states wherein no such certification is provided, unless contrary to local statute, we acknowledge the legitimacy of professionals who: A) Are otherwise qualified under the provisions of items 3.1 and 3.2; and B) would be eligible for certification as a counselor or psychologist in another state.

3.4 We do not consider that participation in one or two workshops on assertive behavior, even though conducted by a professional with an advanced degree, is adequate qualification to offer assertive behavior training to others, unless the additional qualifications of items 3.1 and 3.2 are also met.

3.5 These qualifications are presented as standards for professional facilitators of assertive behavior. No "certification" or "qualifying" agency is hereby proposed. Rather, it is incumbent upon each professional to evaluate himself/herself as a trainer/therapist according to these standards, and to make explicit to clients the adequacy of his/her qualifications as a facilitator.

4. **Ethical Behavior of Facilitators**

Since the encouragement and facilitation of assertive behavior is essentially a therapeutic procedure, the ethical standards most applicable to the practice of assertive behavior training are those of psychologists. We recognize that many persons who practice some form of assertive behavior training are not otherwise engaged in rendering a "psychological" service (for example, teachers, personnel/training directors). But to all, we support the statement of "Ethical Standards for Psychologists" as adopted by the American Psychological Association as the standard of ethical behavior by which assertive behavior training shall be conducted.

We recognize that the methodology employed in assertive behavior training may include a wide range of procedures, some of which are of unproven value. It is the responsibility of facilitators to inform clients of any experimental procedures. Under no circumstances should the facilitator "guarantee" a specific outcome from an intervention.

5. **Appropriateness of Assertive Behavior Training Interventions**

Assertive behavior training, as any intervention oriented toward helping people change, may be applied under a wide range of conditions, yet its appropriateness must be evaluated in each individual case. The responsible selection of assertive behavior training for a particular intervention must include attention to at least the following dimensions:
   A. *Client*: The personal characteristics of the client in question (age, sex, ethnicity, institutionalization, capacity for informed choice, physical and psychological functionality).
   B. *Problem/Goals*: The purpose for which professional help has been sought or recommended (job skills, severe inhibition, anxiety reduction, overcome aggression).
   C. *Facilitator*: The personal and professional qualifications of the facilitator in question (age, sex, ethnicity, skills, understanding, ethics. See also Principles 3 and 4 above).
   D. *Setting*: The characteristics of the setting in which the intervention is conducted

(home, school, business, agency, clinic, hospital, prison). Is the client free to choose? Is the facilitator's effectiveness systematically evaluated?

E. *Time/Duration*: The duration of the intervention. Does the time involved represent a brief word of encouragement, a formal training workshop, an intensive and long-term therapeutic effort?

F. *Method*: The nature of the intervention. Is it "packaged" procedure or tailored to client needs? Is training based on sound principles of learning and behavior? Is there clear differentiation of aggressiveness, assertiveness, and other concepts? Are definitions, techniques, procedures, and purposes clarified? Is care taken to encourage small, successful steps and to minimize punishing consequences? Are any suggested homework assignments presented with adequate supervision, responsibility, and sensitivity to the effect upon significant others of the client's behavior change efforts? Are clients informed that assertiveness doesn't always work?

G. *Outcome*: Are there follow-up procedures, either by self-report or other post-test procedures?

6. **Social Responsibility**

Assertive behavior training shall be conducted within the law. Trainers and clients are encouraged to work assertively to change those laws which they consider need to be changed and to modify the social system in ways they believe appropriate—in particular, to extend the boundaries of human rights. Toward these ends, trainers are encouraged to facilitate responsible change skills via assertive behavior training. All those who practice, teach, or do research on assertive behavior are urged to advocate caution and ethical responsibility in application of the technique in accordance with these principles.